Joseph Berington

The State and Behaviour of English Catholics, from the Reformation to the Year 1780

With a view of their present number, wealth, character, etc. In Two parts.

Joseph Berington

The State and Behaviour of English Catholics, from the Reformation to the Year 1780
With a view of their present number, wealth, character, etc. In Two parts.

ISBN/EAN: 9783337295561

Printed in Europe, USA, Canada, Australia, Japan

Cover: Foto ©Lupo / pixelio.de

More available books at **www.hansebooks.com**

THE
STATE and BEHAVIOUR
OF
ENGLISH CATHOLICS,
FROM
The Reformation to the Year 1780.
WITH
A View of their present Number, Wealth, Character, &c.

IN TWO PARTS.

> Sic nos in luce timemus
> Interdum, nihilo quæ sunt metuenda magis, quam
> Quæ pueri in tenebris pavitant, finguntque futura.
> Lucret.

LONDON:
Printed for R. Faulder, New-Bond-Street.
MDCCLXXX.

PREFACE.

BEFORE the press be closed, I see a propriety in prefixing a few observations. When in manuscript, the following pages were submitted to the inspection of friends; they made objections, which I attended to; and I made some alterations at their request. I could not do all they desired, because I could not totally sacrifice my own ways of thinking. I owed something to myself, as well as to them.

The printed sheets have also been seen by others, whose moderation and improved abilities I greatly value. It is proper, attention should be paid to their remarks. They have told me that,

I should have quoted *authorities* for what, on many occasions, I have said.

My answer is—That my information has been principally taken from well-known sources; from Lord Clarendon, Bishop Burnet, Mr. Hume, and other writers on English History. I wished not to crowd an humble page with the pom-

pous

pous display of great names. It was necessary to read much, but I could collect little. Catholics, for many years back, had made too inconsiderable a figure in the drama of human life, to attract the notice of the annalist or the historian. In the most crouded narratives of English business, they seldom appear, unless where peevish humour brings them forward, for an object of censure or of malignant satyre. There is a *Church History of England, from the year* 1500 *to the year* 1688, published some years ago by a Catholic Clergyman, which was of use to me. It contains many things, regarding Catholics, during that period, extremely curious and well authenticated.——The delineation of modern Catholics was generally drawn from my own observation and experience.

They have told me, I am too animated, too free, and occasionally too severe on all parties; that Catholics may not be pleased, and that Protestants may be offended.

My answer is—If I am *too animated*, it is not my fault. I write as I feel; and the regulating of the state of my nerves is not at my own option. Besides, the view
of

PREFACE.

of many things I had to contemplate, was of a nature sufficiently stimulant to rouse powers much less irritable than mine. After all, dull composition is but a sorry entertainment.—If I write with *freedom*; let it be remembered, I am an Englishman; and though oppressed, my thoughts are not shackled, nor am I tongue-tied. It is a well-known description of a good historian, given by Cicero, when Rome was no longer free, *Ne quid falsi dicere audeat, ne quid veri non audeat*; that is, *Let him dare to speak all truth, let him not dare to tell a lie.*—I do not think I have been too severe on any party. I saw faults on all sides, and those faults I censured. If Catholics be not pleased: They may know, that I did not write with views of pleasing them. I aimed to inform, and if possible, to correct. Lords, Priests, and Commons, now have, and always have had, something in their characters and in their manners, which is reprehensible. They would not wish I should flatter them. If Protestants be offended at any thing I have said, I shall be sorry, because I did not mean to give offence. Do they however suppose, their conduct has not been often extremely censurable?

It has been said——That I generally use the word *Catholic* without the restrictive term *Roman*; and that I studiously avoid the words *Papist* and *Popery*.——It is true, I have intentionally done so. Why should I apply an unnecessary epithet, when the single appellation of *Catholic* sufficiently distinguished the party I was describing? Besides, the word *Roman* has been given us to intimate some *undue* attachment to the See of Rome. *Catholic* is an old family name, which we have never forfeited.—— The words *Popery* and *Papist* are peculiarly insultive. I am no Papist, nor is my Religion Popery. The one and the other have no proper existence, but in the misrepresentations of our adversaries; something of them may perhaps be found in the kingdoms of Italy, Spain, and Portugal.

Such, I think, are the principal objections, which have hitherto reached me: But there is a class of men amongst us, whose opinions I wish to combat.——They are enemies to every species of writing on the business of Catholics. We should not, they say, raise the observation of the public; our security is in our obscurity; if noticed, the law may be called in to lash us

PREFACE. vii

us into silence; what signify charges, however gross and defamatory; it is not possible to remove the national odium; we are now unmolested, who knows how long we may continue so, if we dare to shew our faces?

Such, and much more, is the language of these very prudent, very cautious, very provident, and very timid Gentlemen. Whilst the tumults of last summer were raging in the Metropolis, their voice was heard tremblingly giving counsel: "For God-sake, said they, let us instantly petition parliament to repeal this obnoxious bill; it is better to confess we are guilty of all the crimes laid to our charge, than to be burnt in our houses:" It was *wondrous pitiful*; and they dared to carry about a form of a petition to that effect, praying for the signature of names! "We told you, continued they, what would be the event of your addresses to the throne, your oaths of allegiance, and your repeal of laws."

How far, in certain circumstances, it might be adviseable to keep silence, I will not pretend to say. This I know, it is a conduct

conduct we practised for many years, but from it was never derived any good.—— Silence may be construed into a conviction of guilt, as well as of innocence. Before the repeal of the *Act* of William we were not molested; that is, not perpetually molested, (for there were some very recent instances of signal molestation) but our condition, at all times, was of that debasing and irksome nature, which would have justified the most active exertions. Shall I sit down silently satisfied, because the good humour of a Magistrate chuses to indulge me; whilst there are laws of which any miscreant has daily power to inforce the execution? My ease, my property, and my life are at the disposal of every villain, and I am to be pleased, because he is not at this time disposed to deprive me of them. To-morrow his humour may vary, and I shall then be obliged to hide my head in some dark corner, or to fly from this land of boasted liberty. It is surely better *not to be*, than to live in a state of such anxious and dreadful uncertainty.

However, as the eyes of the public are now open upon us, the reasons which, with

PREFACE.

with some plausibility, might have been urged for silence, subsist no longer. It is now our duty to say, and to do every thing, that can keep up the public attention. The more we are viewed, the more our principles are weighed, and the more our conduct is scrutinized, the more will it appear, that we are deserving of every indulgence. Why is innocence to retire from inspection; and why is merit to fear the prying eye of the severest inquisition? I wish to see every element of our lives and principles most scrupulously analysed; and I will do my utmost to promote the work. I am not sanguine enough to imagine, that it will be in our power to extirpate the national odium, or to stop the cry of malignant defamation: But posterity may feel the good effects of our endeavours. At all events, when men seem cautious to avoid enquiry, a suspicion is raised, either that they fear the result, or that there is something beneath the surface, which they wish not to expose to public inspection.—I would always avoid controversial disputes about religion; because on these subjects every thing has been said, which human ingenuity and zeal for religion could suggest: But as

long

long as the queſtion is, ſhould this or that ſect of Chriſtians be *tolerated* or be *perſecuted*, it is the duty of every man to plead the cauſe of human nature.

I muſt not lay down my pen, without adverting to two recent publications, which I have juſt read: *A Free Addreſs to the Proteſtant Petitioners*, by a *Lover of Peace and Truth*, and Mr. *Burke's Speech* to the Electors of Briſtol.—*The Lover of Peace and Truth* is, I am told, Dr. Prieſtley; the character indeed of the man is ſtrongly marked in the publication; and never was any work better calculated to anſwer the purpoſe for which it was deſigned; it is juſtly levelled to the capacities of thoſe, on whom it was intended to operate; it is plain, honeſt, unadorned, and chriſtian. Nothing can point out more deciſively the extent of Dr. Prieſtley's abilities, than the facility with which he deſcends from the heights of ſcientifical enquiry, to the humble walks of moral inſtruction; in the ſame breath he reads lectures to the Philoſopher, the Divine, and the Stateſman, and he guides the lowly multitude to the practice of domeſtic and ſocial virtue. The tenets of our Church he he indeed treats with too much asperity: It is not the error of his heart; but he pursues, what he esteems the corruptions of religion, with unremitting ardour. I have often conversed with him: He is extremely liberal, and an enemy to every species of restraint on conscience. I blame him for his too free deviations from the received opinions of mankind. By this he has raised up enemies; but all the liberty he takes to himself, he would give in the fullest latitude to others. Had Dr. Priestley no blemishes, he would soar, by the powers of his mind, beyond the reach of common nature; I view, therefore, with malignant satisfaction, the few spots which thinly darken his surface.

Mr. Burke's *Speech*, wherein he replies to the objections that had been made to his parliamentary conduct, is a manly composition. He had been principally blamed for the very decided part he took in the Catholic bill. He meets the charge, in its greatest strength, before his late Constituents; and he tells them, so far from seeing criminality in that conduct, he gloried in what he had done; because, in opposition to fanaticism and intolerant zeal,

b

zeal, he had supported the rights of human nature, and aimed to emancipate a deserving body of fellow-citizens from the iron hand of oppression.—Mr. Burke! *we thank you!* May you be soon restored to those walls, which, in your absence, seem shorn of their brightest beams!

Lucem redde tuæ, Vir bone, patriæ:
Instar veris enim vultus ubi tuus
Affulsit populo, gratior it dies,
    Et soles melius nitent.   HORAT.

With every thinking man it must surely be a proof highly in our favour, that we have not a friend, in either house, whom honour and virtue do not call their friend. When I name the Chancellor, I name the first man in this, or perhaps in any other kingdom: And were I to name all those, who wish to give relief to Catholics, I think I should name whatever this nation has greatest to boast of, in liberality of sentiment, extent of abilities, love of liberty, and ardour to maintain the rights of mankind. Supported by these pillars, it is not possible we can fall; should we fall, ruin thus circumstanced would be more enviable than triumph.

PREFACE.

I have only to beg the indulgence of my readers to the many faults which the following pages will exhibit. I was straitened for time, and my sources of information were scanty. However, I have done my best. Where my language is deficient, the man of candour will recollect that, when eleven years old I was sent to a foreign land for education, and did not return till after almost twenty years of miserable exile.

CARLTON, Dec. 3, 1780.

ERRATA.

Page 8. Line 16. for *would*, read *could*.
P. 31. l. 6. ditto.
P. 43. l. 20. for *refis*, read *reft*.
P. 56. l. 25. after the words, *who knew nothing of the first*, put a full point.
P. 128. l. 1. after *natural*, read *or*.

THE STATE and BEHAVIOUR

OF

ENGLISH CATHOLICS

FROM THE

REFORMATION to the present Year 1780.

PART I.

INTRODUCTION.

THE riots which, some months ago, threatened destruction to the Capital of the British Empire, and the debates consequent thereupon in both houses of parliament, have given rise to much speculation. It is obvious to enquire, from whence such commotions could have arisen. Under the popular cry, *No Popery*, an *Association* had been formed; and the members of this association were the ostensible agents in the confusion and devastation which succeeded. Was then an apprehension

A

Introduction prehension of the *increase* of Popery, from the indulgence Catholics had lately received, the real instrument which convened the *Associators*, and which produced their tumultuous application to parliament? I am ready to believe that much of the evil which was done, in the demolition of private and of national property, was merely accidental; that it was effected by the horrid activity of such miscreants, as are ever ready, under the screen of popular commotion, to practise their bad designs. Where no sufficient ground is given for fair supposition, it would be wrong to infer any preconcerted plan for general destruction. Some years hence, perhaps, we may be better able to form a judgment.—I am also ready to allow, that the *Protestant Association* might be influenced by motives, to them of a cogent and weighty nature. They might seriously apprehend, from a supposed increase of *Popery*, that danger threatened the established Church, and the civil Constitution of Great Britain. It became their duty therefore to take the alarm, and to petition for the repeal of an obnoxious act.—In reasoning on a dark subject, I am willing to make all allowances that the circumstances of things, or

the

the operation of human passions, can justify.

From a general view indeed of the characters of those men, who formed the *Protestant Association*, it will be more rational, I believe, to conclude, that they had no distinct object before them: For they were not qualified to combine ideas, or to project schemes of operation. To all appearance there never was so illiterate and rude a multitude: But their minds, open to every impression, had been struck by an artful description of imaginary evils; and they followed blindly every impulse of their leaders. What were the views of these men, I pretend not to say: Perhaps they also were seriously apprehensive; or perhaps, (which I should rather suspect to be the case) under the cover of fictitious dread, and of vain solicitude for the good of religion, they had formed their designs, in which ambition or disappointed passion had a leading interest. But I wish not to hazard a decided opinion.

It is a reflection not easily reconcileable with the present advanced state of the human mind; however, I am much disposed

Introduction to believe that it was the dread alone of Popery which instigated the Associators. The records of bigotry and fanaticism will ever occupy a large space in the annals of mankind. A person but little acquainted with the general sentiments of Englishmen, in the business of religion, will be necessitated to draw the same conclusion. There still remains in the mind of almost every Protestant, from the highest to the lowest, from the best-informed to the most ignorant, from the infidel to the zealot, and from the fanatic to the man of cool reason, a rooted prejudice against the name of *Catholic*, which no time, I fear, or the efforts of philosophy, will ever erase. No sooner is the infant mind susceptible of the slightest impression, than it is the business of the nurse to paint a hideous form, and that she calls *Popery*. Every circumstance of horror, and all the scenery of glowing imagination, is called in to deck the curious phantom. Nor afterwards is it the aim of better judgment to remove this false impression; rather all the arts of declamation are sedulously employed to give it a more fixed and lasting permanency. Few men, I believe, are strangers to the inveterate obstinacy of such early notions.

At

Introduction

At the beginning of what is called the *Reformation*, it was natural to expect that the old religion, against which such mighty designs were formed, would be held out, by the new apostles, in colours best calculated to rouse every idea of distaste and detestation. To have engaged in so arduous a work, without such assistance, would have been the extreme of folly. Fortunately for their designs, the general corruption which had long prevailed over the face of Christianity, afforded too abundant matter for censure; and this circumstance the Reformers well knew how to turn to their own advantage. They wilfully confounded abuses in *practice* with abuses in *belief*; asserting that the Christian faith had been corrupted, when they knew the adjuncts, that is, the inventions of men only were bad; and thus forcibly blending together objects so really distinct, they ungenerously drew a representation full of horror, on which rose the whole fabric of the reformed religion.—Though I highly condemn the conduct of the first Reformers, it is not my intention to cast censure on the Protestants of the present day: The cause is entirely their own: Nor is it at all my wish to enter into controversial dispute.

The

Introduction The Christian world has wrangled too long. But if the declaration of historical truth give offence, it is a proof that it has not been sufficiently urged.

I wish to contemplate the revolutions in Church and State, with the cool indifference of philosophy. On every side may be discovered many traces of similar passions; and very few events there are in either, wherein reason and the amiable influence of virtue had any leading concern. That great revolution, by which Christianity was introduced, is always to be excepted.—I allow, however, that much good was *eventually* derived to the Christian Church from the Reformation. The professors of the old religion were roused to more active virtue; they saw the necessity of proper discrimination betwixt human inventions and divine institutions; and a spirit of universal enquiry was soon set on foot, the happy effects of which are now experienced. But the Reformers might have aimed at the correction of abuses, without touching, with profane hands, the vital substance; or surely they might have proceeded in a spirit of more moderation, and with less appearance of passion and

and interested zeal. Had they done so, their names had gone down with more reverence to the grave; and we should not now have to lament those feuds and deep animosities which have for ever divided the Christian world.

More than two centuries are now elapsed since the first days of Reformation. It was natural to expect that long ago all that rancour and heated recrimination would have subsided, which first animated the contending parties. When the *Sectaries* had firmly established themselves; that is, when their opinions had taken fast hold, had new-modelled the political constitutions of many kingdoms, and had made with them one connected and almost indissoluble mass, they had nothing, it seems, farther to apprehend. The policy therefore of representing *Popery*, with a hundred heads and a hundred arms, ready to devour and to destroy, subsisted no longer. Yet still the same arts of imposition were used, and always with the same success.—It cannot indeed be denied but fresh incentives were soon added to keep up the acrimony of old impressions, and many of these were of a complexion really alarming

Introduction ing. The barbarities practised by the Catholics on many, whose sole crime often was difference in belief, cannot be too much execrated; and the blood of innocence, which was then spilled, became the seed of fatal animosities. In those wars, indeed, in which whole provinces, and even kingdoms were engaged, and wherein, under the veil of zeal for religion, crimes of every description were perpetrated, equal blame, it seems, may be justly cast on both sides. It was often the bad policy of states, or the intemperate pretensions of faction, which gave rise to these contentions: Religion at least could have no concern, though her sacred name was for ever blasphemed.—The unprejudiced man, if such a one there be, in perusing the annals of those bad days, will find abundant matter for indiscriminate reprehension; and he will close the page equally shocked and equally exasperated at the conduct of all parties.

ON a review of the transactions of my own country, in matters of religion, (for I wish to confine myself within these limits) it is not difficult, I think, to form a decided and just opinion. The Reformation was here introduced by means the most violent and oppressive. The tyrant Henry could use no other. Deprived of their property, persecuted in their persons, and defamed in their reputation, could it be expected that *English* Catholics would, in silence, forsake the religion of their forefathers, however erroneous it had been, or, without reluctance, bow their heads to oppression? He indeed must be peculiarly clear-sighted who, through this whole reign, can discover, in any one instance, the genuine spirit of Christian Reformation. It was not, at least, by such means that primitive Christianity was established; though I know it is sometimes by pestilence and by storms that the benevolent designs of Providence are conducted. But I mean not to dwell longer on the events of this reign, when the cause of Catholics was the common cause of the nation. Moderate men are little inclined to give credit to the report

Henry VIII. of numberless crimes and flagitious enormities, of which they were accused; because the views of his Majesty and the rapacity of Courtiers wanted such a plea in vindication of their conduct.

Edward VI. DURING the short period of Edward's reign, the work of Reformation went on, gradually acquiring form and permanency. Less severity was sometimes used, than the nation had before experienced; but moderation, at these times, was an unknown virtue. I would rather leave my friend in error, than make him a proselyte to truth by such means.—At the death of the late King, things were in great confusion; the old religion had been violently shaken, but the tenets of the new one were neither established nor even publicly known. Henry himself had been really no friend to the Reformers; impetuosity of temper had alone driven him to such outrageous attacks on a religion he interiorly reverenced; and by his last will he solemnly ordained, and charges all his successors to take care, that *Masses* be daily said in the Chapel at Windsor, *while the world shall endure.*—

The

The friends to the *Reformation* saw the necessity of taking effectual measures. Great part of the Nobility, many of the Gentry, and the Bishops with the inferior Clergy, were still much attached to the ancient form of worship. The protector *Somerset*, and *Cranmer*, that ductile and time-serving Priest, almost singly engaged in the holy work, and they succeeded. All opposition was weak against the excessive power of such crafty and formidable Ministers. Some fruitless attempts were made; but it now appeared, that the establishment of the new religion, was the only means of securing to the first occupiers the possession of the Church-wealth they had already laid their hands on; it would also open a door to new acquisitions from the same quarter. This it was, and not love for religion, that so well promoted the reforming scheme—and not only the revenues of the Church, but the libraries also, underwent a dreadful scrutiny. Those of Westminster and Oxford were ordered to be ransacked, and purged of all Romish superstition. Many of the most valuable books, even of human literature, were plated with gold and silver. " This, as far as

Edward VI. we can guess, says Collier, was the superstition which destroyed them." Works of Geometry and Astronomy were at once known to contain magic, this was rank Popery; and they threw them into the flames. The universities, unable to stop the fury of these worthy Reformers, silently looked on, and trembled for their own security.

Mary. AS I condemn the boisterous violence of Henry, and the unpopular and gothic conduct of Edward's Ministers, so do I condemn the proceedings of Mary, who, by ways equally reprehensible, aimed to restore what her father and infant brother had overthrown. They, and their Counsellors, were alike strangers to the dictates of reason and to the genuine principles of true religion. Yet it cannot seem strange, if such Catholics as had remained firmly attached to the old worship, eagerly embraced the first occasion of reinstating themselves. In so doing passion would too often intervene; nor was it an easy task to refrain from some retaliation, while the wounds they had received were fresh and bleeding.—But nothing surely can be more uncandid than the reflections of Protestants, when they speak of these times. They can ascribe the mad conduct of Henry to the impulse of violent passion; but in Mary they pretend to see nothing but a mind contracted, as they say, by the bigoted and sanguinary principles of her religion. I hate a man thus miserably partial to his own cause.

Mary.

It is worth notice, that Sir Thomas Wyatt, who headed a formidable insurrection against Mary, was himself a Catholic. A treaty of marriage had been concluded betwixt the Queen and Philip of Spain. No step, it was judged, could be better calculated to support the cause of Catholicity; but it was by some feared that England had much reason to be jealous of so close a connexion with a crown, whose great ambition now aimed at universal monarchy: Hurried on by an impulse of rash patriotism, Wyatt therefore rose in arms. The love of country outweighed every other consideration.

IN the year 1558, Elizabeth ascended the throne of England. At this time begins

Elizabet

Elizabeth. gins the real era of English Reformation; and consequently from this time Catholics are to be considered as a sect, dissenting from the national Church.—To enter on a minute detail of the many events, in the line of religious politics, which rapidly succeeded one another, during this long reign, would carry me too far; but I shall not willingly omit any circumstance which can serve to mark the real character of Catholics. The most rigorous penal laws were now enacted against them, and they were carried into execution under various pretences. They were accused of sedition, and of engaging in the most unremitted attempts against the person of their Sovereign and the established religion, with a view to introduce a Popish successor, and, on the ruins of Protestantism, to re-establish the Catholic faith. I will not say that no Catholics were ever guilty of these crimes. It could not possibly be otherwise: for they were men, and they had the passions of men. What man, when he either thinks himself ill-used, or really is so, will not strive to gain redress? *Un ver de terre se resent, quand on lui marche*, said, at this time, a much-injured Princess, in a letter addressed to her cruel persecutrix: But the body

of

of Catholics, which was then very confiderable, never engaged in, and never encouraged, any fchemes of fedition or treafon. Yet, furely, no condition was ever more humiliating than theirs; and if they did not ardently look forward to any event that might give them relief, oppreffion muft have deadened every feeling of nature!

Plots, whether real or fictitious, in the hands of an able politician, are thofe fortunate engines, which he will know how to turn to every poffible ufe. The darknefs in which they are involved fupplies the greateft latitude of interpretation. If *real*, as plots are feldom attended with fuccefs, the arm of government will be ftrengthened by their detection, and notice will be given for the application of fuch remedies as may feem neceffary to the fupport of the ftate. Its defects or weak parts are now laid open. The heads of feditious intrigue will either be taken off, or will be fecured againft further attempts: Faction will be broken. The ruling powers have then acquired a more firm and extenfive energy.—*Fictitious* plots are attended with ftill greater advantages. By
their

Elizabeth. their means some devoted party may be marked out, and be consigned to a fatal and national odium. At that moment the statesman's hand is armed with a potent wand, whereby he will be able to conjure up all the spirits of the deep. He will gratify his creatures with the forfeited spoils of the unhappy sufferers; private animosities will find room for the exertion of resentment; revenge and all the passions of interest will know no bounds. In the mean-time the attention of the credulous and unsuspecting multitude is caught; an impression is made; and their minds are raised to the view of dreadful dangers and imaginary horrors.—The crafty minister will probably seize this critical hour for carrying into execution some favourite and unpopular design.

Such phantom-plots are with us no new device. We may see them practised in every reign: But the Catholics of England, from the time of the Reformation, have felt their fatal effects in fullest measure. The religion they professed was directly contrary to the statutes of the nation: Being compelled to seek for education in foreign countries, they easily fell under suspicions

suspicions of being in the interest of those Princes, who had given them protection: They admitted, as a part of their religious belief, a certain supremacy of jurisdiction in the Roman Pontiff, which, though in itself no real cause of jealousy, was then often misconceived, and sometimes very improperly exercised; in a word, they were oppressed, and therefore not without reason suspected of an habitual inclination to shake off the galling chain, whenever occasion should offer. Thus circumstanced, the condition of Catholics became a common repertory, from whence it was easy to draw such plot-materials, as the views of party or the situation of things seemed most to require.

Their condition was not intolerably grievous till the year 1569, the 11th of Elizabeth, when the misbehaviour of a few men drew a persecution on the whole body, and occasioned those penal and sanguinary laws, to which their property and lives have been ever since exposed. From that time, by a strange perversion of the common rules of reasoning, a *Catholic* and a *Rebel* have been viewed as synonymous objects; and infamy was stamped on the name.—

Elizabeth. name.—An insurrection, under the Earls of Northumberland and Westmorland, two Catholic Peers, was raised in the North. Discontented from various causes, but under pretence of redressing the public grievances, and of supporting the old religion, they took up arms. They were joined by a considerable body of their dependents and northern friends: but the Catholics of the other parts of the kingdom, as our best historians agree, publicly declared against them, and loyally offered their lives and their purses for the defence of her Majesty. The rebellion was soon crushed; but government had now an handle given them, the Catholics were doomed to destruction, and the laws of the 13th of Elizabeth were framed against them.

By these acts, religion and civil allegiance were so artfully blended, that an impeachment in either served both purposes; and a constant fund was established for the manufacturing of plots, when the national politics called for a stratagem. An occasion soon offered. A treaty of marriage had been for some time carried on between the Queen and the French Duke of Anjou. Ministry disliked the alliance, and the subtle

subtle Walsingham was resolved to obstruct it. It might be prejudicial to the Reformation; or at least it might procure some toleration for Catholics. The determination was to make the Duke odious to the English nation. A rumour was spread abroad of a deep design. It was said, that in the Colleges at Rheims and Rome, to which places the Catholics had been compelled to retire for education, a plot had been formed to subvert the government, and to destroy the Queen. To accomplish this grand purpose, the Priests had engaged themselves by a solemn oath before the Bishop of Rome.—Never was there a more groundless charge; for I do not find, that it possessed one single atom of the most distant truth. But the Minister had provided himself with a miscreant band of witnesses, who were ready for any work. Their names and characters are upon record. Hypocritical, indigent, and abandoned, they had not the smallest remains of reputation left amongst them. The nation was, however, well disposed to give credit. Some Priests were found guilty, condemned, and executed. This, says Camden, was a politic stroke; the apprehensions of a great many were appeased;

Elizabeth. sed; and the ferment about the Duke of Anjou subsided. The alliance, they said, had threatened ruin to the Protestant Religion.—Few years passed afterwards without the execution of one or more Churchmen of the Catholic persuasion. They were held out to the people as traitors; and such indeed they were; for the laws had now declared the profession of their religion to be Treason against the State.

The next designs, of a seditious nature, with which Catholics were charged, were of being concerned in Babington's plot in the year 1586, and in the great Spanish Armament two years after.——A few Gentlemen, about fourteen in number, of moderate fortunes, and of some interest in their neighbourhood, fired at the ignominious treatment, which the amiable Mary had so long experienced from the hands of Elizabeth, resolved to attempt the rescue of the Captive Queen. There was one priest in the conspiracy. Walsingham was well apprised of their whole scheme, and he had his spies amongst them sedulously employed to urge on the execution. When the plot was ripe for discovery, it was not difficult to seize the delinquents: Their names,

names, haunts, and places of abode were all known to the Minister. At their examination they were charged with the design of attempting to release the Scottish Queen, encouraging an invasion, and assassinating their Sovereign. They were condemned and executed.——The Duke of Norfolk, a Protestant, had some years before engaged in a similar project, as far at least as it regarded the release of Mary, whom he loved. He also had suffered.—— If we except the conspirators themselves, no other Catholics were engaged in the plot, or at all acquainted with it; yet occasion was taken to put the laws against them into severer execution. Mary herself was soon after brought to the block, and Elizabeth was freed from a hated rival. Her chief guilt was flagrant: She was in possession of some personal charms, which nature had denied to the English Queen. Mary had a finer shape; her countenance was more expressive; and her step in dancing, it is said, was more graceful. Elizabeth could not brook this partial indulgence of nature: the sceptre of England was hardly worth possessing, if she were not also thought the Queen of Beauty. Mary had no other crime; for surely it

could

Elizabeth. could be no crime, after twenty years severe confinement, to have concerted with Babington the best measures for the recovery of her liberty! If the Conspirators had really formed any design of seizing and of assassinating their own Sovereign, which I do not think they ever did, it was undoubtedly flagitious; but scarcely more so, than was the design of Elizabeth and her friends against the life of Mary of Scotland. At all events, how could Catholics be charged with an attempt, in which they had no concern? As well might the Protestants of England have been accused of treasonable practices, because a Duke of their religion, with some associates of the same persuasion, had embarked in a scheme, which had been construed into treason. Norfolk wished to deliver, and then to present his hand to Mary; the less interested Babington had no views but to rescue her from captivity. And this was a crime for which the Catholics of England were to be devoted to destruction!

In regard to the intended invasion from Spain, we were, if possible, still less concerned than in the plot just mentioned. The

The Conspirators were Catholics: But the *Invincible Armada* had no claim to their friendship; unless, because Catholics professed the religion of the invaders, they must be supposed to have abetted their design. The Spanish *Manifesto* declares the motives of this expedition: It was to chastise the English for the assistance they had given to the rebels in the Netherlands; to retaliate for the many depredations committed by them on the coasts of Spain and America; and to revenge the insult which had been offered to the dignity of all crowned heads by the barbarous murder of Mary Queen of Scots. Some views of a religious tendency might also have intervened, but they constituted no leading object. To the English Catholics no application had been made for their concurrence; on the contrary, the Spanish Monarch refused to employ those few Catholic soldiers of fortune who were then in his dominions; for though they eat their bread from his table, he durst not, he said, trust them in any attempt against England. Yet did this formidable expedition prove more unfortunate to the Catholic party, than it did to the English nation. Providence

conspiring

Elizabeth. conspiring with British valour, the Armada was sunk and dissipated; when Elizabeth, in imitation of those ancient nations, I suppose, who delighted in the practice, resolved to return thanks to the Deity in a sacrifice of human victims. The Catholics were ordered over to a general prosecution; great numbers were imprisoned, and above forty Priests were publicly butchered in several parts of the kingdom; whilst the pulpit and the press were employed in representing them as the authors and abettors of the intended invasion. I have before me a faithful narrative of the trials of those who suffered; and if any confidence can be placed in the solemn protestations of dying men, I venture to declare, there was not the smallest guilt amongst them.

On all these public occasions, the English Catholics being clear from any imputation of real guilt, the attempts of particular persons, either against the Queen or her government, cannot, with the least semblance of equity, be laid to their charge. Hard indeed would be the fate of mankind, if whole societies were made answerable for the criminal conduct of a few

few of their members! Yet so, I think, it sometimes was during the reign of Elizabeth. Occasion being taken from the events I have mentioned, a code of laws, as has been seen, was made against Catholics. By these their property, liberty, and lives became obnoxious to prosecution. To worship God, after the old form, was prohibited in public and in private; and the prisons were filled with Delinquents, whose sole crime was praying in the manner their consciences directed. They were not allowed to educate their children in the schools at home, unless they renounced their religion; and to send them abroad was made a crime of the most heinous nature. Their foreign schools were termed nurseries of rebellion. They were excluded not only from all places of public trust; but were not even permitted to improve their parts or their private fortunes by the practice of law or physic. Their families were thus reduced to the lowest circumstances, and some of the best blood in England was devoted to beggary; yet to move more than five miles from the sad spot, where their ancestors had lived in ease and splendor, was even forbid under the

Elizabeth. severest penalties. To receive the order of Priesthood abroad, to exercise any spiritual functions in her Majesty's dominions, to be reconciled to the ancient faith, or even to assist in such a reconciliation, were by an English parliament, at the end of the sixteenth century, constituted acts of high treason against the state!—Such, in a general view, were the laws framed against Catholics in a Protestant country; yet I will take it upon me to assert that, during the long period of forty four years, whilst Elizabeth, to the great political glory of England, swayed the Sceptre, her Popish subjects, though oppressed and persecuted were not guilty of *one act* of treason, sedition, or rebellion.

I have taken no notice of the famous Bull of Pius the Fifth, which excommunicated Elizabeth, and absolved her subjects from their allegiance, because it was never accepted by the English Catholics; nor was it ever signified to them in any legal or canonical manner: It had not therefore the least influence on their conduct. They universally acknowledged her title; prayed for her; fought for her; and upon every occasion were ready to support her dignity and defend her *civil* rights. They only did not think her the *spiritual* head of their church.— The power of deposing Princes which Pius assumed, and which other Pontiffs had before him often exercised, was a part of that prerogative, which arrogant ambition had usurped, and which, for a long time, the weakness or ignorance of mankind durst not infringe. Purer notions of religion, and improved politics, have now taught the See of Rome more moderation and better maxims.

Elizabeth.

IN 1603, James the First was called to the throne of England. This was an event which the Catholics had long ardently wished for, and on it they had built the most sanguine expectations. From the natural mildness of his temper, from the favours he had received from Catholic Princes, and from a recollection, which was not effaced, of the warm attachment they had ever shewn for his mother, they certainly had reason to expect more humane treatment and some marks of indulgence. James was a friend to toleration;

James I.

James I.

ration; he wished to conciliate all parties; he had studied religion; and he well knew, from repeated trials of their untractable humour, that he had much more to fear from the Disciples of Calvin, than from the Catholics of any country. The doctrines of those men had now acquired an extensive influence; and the established Church began already to feel their impression. "Let men be punished for actions, said he, and not for opinions." It was a just observation, but it gave offence. The ruling party alone thought they had a claim to protection.——The English Ministry were aware of his favourable disposition to Catholics, and they strove to avert its effects. He was therefore prevailed on, soon after his arrival, to issue a proclamation for banishing all Jesuits and Seminary Priests; and a statute was also enacted, ordering the penal laws of Elizabeth to be put in execution. It is, however, well known that he did not mean things should proceed to extremities. The Stuarts had not in their composition one fibre of that stern texture, which had marked the Tudor race of Kings;

Kings; but it was no easy task to manage the testy humour of the nation.

Great was the disappointment of the Catholic party, when they saw at once all their bright schemes of happiness dashed in pieces, and themselves again exposed to severity and oppression. The King, they saw, however well disposed, either wanted fortitude or power to befriend them; and the Puritans, from whom they had every thing to dread, were daily gaining strength and energy. Nothing therefore remained but to resign themselves to a fate they could not avert; and to this they silently submitted.

In every society will be found men of restless dispositions, of desperate fortunes, and of daring character. Such there now were amongst the Catholics; and by them was concerted one of the most determined, but most wild and nefarious schemes, ever heard of in the annals of any nation. This was the *gunpowder plot*: By which, had it succeeded, the King and both houses of parliament had been destroyed at one blow. The fifth of November, 1605, the third year of his

James I. his Majesty's reign, was the day appointed for its execution. Providence again singularly interfered, and the nation was saved from so dreadful a catastrophe.

The spirit of desperation, or of complete wickedness, seems alone to have planned this grand scheme of destruction. In no part are discoverable any views of policy; no project of a revolution had been formed; no foreign invasion was ready to second their attempts; their own party, that is, the party of Catholics, was not apprised; nor had they prepared any one measure for further operations. The Conspirators, when most numerous, including their servants, did not exceed eighty; and above twenty Catholic Peers sat, at that time, in the upper house, who surely were not acquainted with the design. A report had indeed been privately circulated, that something, they knew not what, was in agitation for the good of Catholicity.——If the Conspirators really intended to serve their brethren, never was there a more misjudged project: For, in either case, of success or detection, their ruin was inevitable.——It has been by some thought

thought that the enemies to the Catholics, apprehensive of the King's favourable dispositions to them, had a principal hand in the plot; and that Cecil well understood its whole rise and progress. So much at least is certain, that no event would have happened so agreeable to the views of their enemies, or so dreadfully fatal to the Catholic cause. Its effects are very sensibly felt to this day. A feast was politically instituted to perpetuate its memory; to the Catholics was imputed its whole atrocity: nor has the fullest evidence of their innocence contributed to wipe off the foul aspersion; or their most solemn protestations been able to remove the imputation, that they are prone to sedition, foes to public tranquillity, and fond of blood. Yet the moderate part of the nation, which unfortunately was but small, did not then think them guilty; and the King, in his proclamation for apprehending the Conspirators, declares it to have been the design only of a few desperate men.

James I.

The hatred of the nation against Catholics now knew no bounds; and nothing but the utter extinction of that devoted party seemed capable of satisfying their rage.

James I. rage. James alone, with a becoming resolution, though it was not his usual conduct, rejected all measures of violence, and was the protector of innocence. Yet again he consented to new laws against *Popish Recusants*, which are those of the third of James. I am shocked at the view of such infamous proceedings; nor do I wish to disguise my feelings. A few miscreants had engaged in an infamous confederacy, in which the multitude had no participation, and which they execrated; yet are the latter also punished, and handed down to posterity in the darkest colours of guilt!

Two years after this wretched event, with a view to ascertain the real sentiments of Catholics, (at least in the intentions of the King) a scheme was set on foot, which seemed well calculated to answer the purpose. An *oath of allegiance*, it was said, would be a proper test of the sincerity of their declarations. An oath was consequently prepared; but it was drawn up in terms, either from design or ignorance, which were likely to raise difficulties, and to perplex the tender consciences of the best disposed. If ministry meant it, their
views

views were completely answered.—It should seem, as if they who framed it (a shrewd Priest and Archbishop Bancroft) well knew where principally lay the point of nicety; and that they wished rather to divide, than to conciliate, the party. As soon as it was proposed, great disputes arose about the lawfulness of the oath: By some it was approved, and taken, whilst others, equally well inclined in their political sentiments, considered it as insidiously worded, and as bearing hard on tenets, in which they thought religion was concerned. The Nonjurors, who were far most numerous, were by these means exposed to daily vexations; and occasion was given for misrepresenting them as disaffected persons, whose professions of attachment to the civil establishment were not to be trusted. Appearances, in the eye of the nation, were now certainly against them; but it is a truth, that no people could be more firmly attached to King and Government, than Catholics then were; but they were disturbed with difficulties, which at this time make no impression. To complete the business, the Roman Pontiff, ever jealous of any attack on his supposed prerogative, very inopportunely interfered, and wholly

James I. wholly fruſtrated a ſcheme, the ſucceſs of which, delicacy of conſcience alone had at firſt obſtructed.

During the remaining part of this reign, no material alteration took place in the affairs of Catholics. No new ſeverities were practiſed, or laws enacted, againſt them; but thoſe already made were occaſionally put in execution; for I have before me a liſt of thirteen Prieſts who were hanged for the exerciſe of their ſacerdotal functions. Every attempt the King made to mitigate the ſeverity of theſe laws, or to give relief to his Catholic ſubjects, was loudly oppoſed, and he was accuſed of being very improperly diſpoſed to favour them.——Whilſt the marriage treaty betwixt his Son and the Infanta of Spain was going on, in the year 1623, ſome ſecret articles were propoſed, and James ſeemed determined to proſecute his favourite plan for general toleration. This, however, was warmly oppoſed by Abbot and others of the Puritanical faction; and as the treaty ſoon broke off, the Catholics were unrelieved.——In this year a flaming petition, from both houſes of parliament, againſt *Popiſh Recuſants*, was preſented to the

the King, praying for the moſt active execution of the laws againſt them. They had been charged with no new crime; but James had allowed them to breathe with ſome liberty, and this, in their eſtimation, was too great an indulgence. "Such an execution of juſtice, ſaid they, will much advance the glory of Almighty God." Theſe men ſhould have been High Prieſts to Moloch, in the vale of Hinnom. The King ſaw into the ſpirit which had dictated this petition. He anſwered by profeſſing his warmeſt attachment to the Proteſtant religion; that he would cautiouſly guard againſt any undue relaxation of the laws; but that "like a good horſeman, he muſt be allowed ſometimes to uſe the reins, and not always the ſpurs.—I am an enemy, continued he, to perſecution; and have ever thought that no way more increaſed any religion than perſecution; ſanguis martyrum eſt ſemen Eccleſiæ."— James was a divine as well as a politician. He died the year following.

James I.

Charles I. ON the accession of Charles, the Catholics were again in some expectation of ease, from his marriage with Henrietta, Princess of France. She was daughter to the great and good Henry the Fourth, and had been educated in a court which had long experienced the direful effects of religious discord. It was therefore hoped she might bring peace to the contending factions of England. Apprehensive of so enviable an event, the jealousy of the Puritans was roused to a more active exertion. These were the men who now began to take the lead in all public affairs; and the young King's court, says Burnet, was full of them. They demanded the execution of the penal laws. A proclamation to this effect was issued; and, in the year 1627, a severe statute was enacted, conformable to the first of James, repeating the prohibition of foreign education. Certain officers, named *Pursuivants*, were likewise appointed, who had almost an unlimited power to enter the houses of Catholics, and to distress them at will. The most groundless rumours were raised, and industriously circulated. The Papists, it was said, were forming, I know not what plot,

plot, againſt the King and Archbiſhop Laud; they were creating a miſunderſtanding betwixt his Majeſty and the parliament; and they were inſtigating the Scots to attempt the ruin of the eſtabliſhed Church! Theſe were bold calumnies; but they had their effect: For, under this diſguiſe, the real promoters of ſedition were ſcreened from obſervation, whilſt the guilt was aſcribed to a party, which had been long the object of popular odium. The Puritans thus played an artful game: Had they made an open attack on Church and State, the nation might have taken a timely alarm; but conducting their deep ſcheme under the ſhow of oppoſing the encroachments of Popery, their ſucceſs was certain. The friends to Charles and to their country ſaw, at laſt, the full tendency of theſe machinations; but it was then too late to ſtem the raging torrent.—In this manner, during the ſixteen firſt years of his Majeſty's reign, was the kingdom perpetually haraſſed with the cry of *Popery*; and no ſituation could be more diſtreſſing than that of the Catholics. Guilty of no one crime, they were accuſed of all. Some conſolation indeed they might draw

from

Charles I. from the reflexion, that as they were principally hated by the ruling faction, it was obvious they were well affected to the King, and friends to religion and virtue.

When the rebellion began, though now there was little want of disguise, yet the same methods were invariably practised. Pym, at the opening of the Long Parliament in the year 1640, among the grievances which he enumerated, complained loudly of the suspension of the laws against Popery; and among other acts of royal power, which this Parliament soon assumed, they issued orders for demolishing all images, altars, and crucifixes. It was the crown, however, and the mitre which these zealous men principally aimed at. Crosses were then removed from the streets and markets; and no two pieces of wood or stone, says an ingenious writer, were permitted to lie quietly over each other at right angles. Alarms of the most shocking nature were propagated: Meetings, it was reported, were held by the Papists in immense caves in Surrey. These caves did not exist, but the belief of them was the same.

A Plot of a singular tendency was devised: London and Westminster were to sink in one common ruin. The Papists, therefore, had laid vast trains of gunpowder to blow up the Thames. Fortunately the powder got wet, and the lives of his Majesty's Protestant subjects were saved from destruction!—When the King went down to the house to demand the five members he had accused of treason, this breach of privilege, as it was called, was ascribed to the bloody counsels of Papists. And when, a few days after, he retired to Hampton-Court, a petition from the apprentices and porters warned the house of the danger to which their religion was exposed; whilst a brewer's wife, followed by many thousands of her sex, also brought up a petition, expressing in the strongest language their terrors of Popery!

When the royal army took the field, the cry of Popery was echoed through the kingdom. "His Majesty, said the Rebels in their declaration, seduced by wicked counsellors, has raised a great army of Papists to destroy the parliament, and to bring in Popery and Tyranny."

The

Charles I. The Catholics indeed were firm in the royal cause; but their personal services were not accepted, till such time as the parliament had itself offered them commissions in their own army. This being known, Charles disregarding all further imputation of being popishly inclined, invited them to his standard. They received commissions to raise companies and regiments. This they did at their own expence, bringing along with them their sons, tenants, and neighbours: Nor, from the fight at Edgehill till the day of the *restoration*, did they ever desert the royal party.—I have now before me a list of six Lieutenant-Generals, eighteen Colonels, sixteen Lieutenant-Colonels, sixteen Majors, sixty nine Captains, fourteen Lieutenants, five Cornets, and fifty Gentlemen Volunteers, of the Catholic persuasion, who lost their lives in defence of his Majesty and of the established constitution in Church and State. The severest oppression, to which, for almost a century, they had been constantly exposed, had not been able to extinguish in their breasts the spirit of real patriotism.

After

After the fatal defeat at Worcester, in 1651, when all the royal party was either killed, taken, or dispersed, the young Charles was successively, for the space of six whole days, in the hands of more than fifty Catholics, not one of whom, either from fear of punishment or from prospect of gain, could be prevailed on to betray their Prince. Yet many of these were in very low condition. The name of Pendrel will be ever memorable in the annals of Loyalty.

Charles I.

THE Commonwealth being established, (as by the subversion of the regal and episcopal order, the grand object of pursuit, was finally settled) the cry against Popery seemed to subside, and the Catholics became confounded in the common mass of those who were thought enemies to the new form of government. What they now suffered was more on account of loyalty than of religion. To conciliate the affections of all men was with Cromwell a leading object; he well knew it was only by such means that his usurped authority could stand. Though no step could have proved more disagreeable to the enthusiasm of his party; yet it appears he had serious thoughts

The Commonwealth.

thoughts of granting a general toleration in religion. Had he done so, and then supported his measures with all that firmness of which he was master, perhaps the Commonwealth of England might have stood to this day. Cromwell had a conference with some few of the Catholic persuasion; they were unauthorized, I find, by their brethren; but, induced by the general aspect of affairs, they thought it good policy to make the best provision for themselves. Sincerity was not one of the Protector's virtues; at all events, he required from those Gentlemen such oaths and engagements, as they were not inclined to accept. In the general body of Catholics there ever remained a stern spirit of loyalty, which no threats or allurements could vanquish. The Protestants of the same faction were equally steady. Yet by some writers Catholics have been represented as deserters from the cause: It has been said, they made their court to the Usurper. It was the wish, perhaps, of these men to screen, if possible, what they thought the wrong behaviour of some of their own friends, by criminating the innocent. Even Clarendon very roundly insinuates the same charge against the Catholics.

tholics. I am confident he knew it was not so, at least in an extensive application: But it should seem, as if the noble author were jealous that the praise of loyalty, of which himself had so ample a share, should be given to a party, whom he never liked. It is not from any romantic ideas of the virtue of loyalty that I say this; for I really think that Catholics, as matters then stood, would have done well to have joined the Protector, had he given them certain assurances of support. They had experienced how little was to be expected from the bounty of Kings; and besides, with the approbation of the major part of the nation, the form of government was altered; consequently the criminality of rebellion was done away. My views then in representing the uniform adhesion of Catholics to King Charles rest solely on the conviction of its truth. In other respects, I am not ashamed to say, that the government which is best inclined to give us protection, has the only right to demand our allegiance.

AT the *Restoration*, in the year 1660, an august and splendid scene opened upon the nation, in the blessings of which Catholics had again reason to expect a participation. It was the King's first wish to grant indulgence to the Protestant Dissenters. This he had solemnly promised before his embarkation for England: he had besides much reason to fear the turbulence of their minds, unless it should be appeased by some favourable concessions. The parliament, now outrageously loyal, opposed every attempt for their relief: They wished to see the Church of England restored to its primitive splendor; and they wished to cast down the aspiring thoughts of the Sectaries. Charles, however, from motives of the best policy, was determined to be their friend.

Nothing was at first done for the Catholics; yet their pretensions were great, and they seemed to look for a proportionable indulgence. "It was the King's desire, says Clarendon, which he never dissembled, to give them ease from all the sanguinary laws." Without importunity or complaint, had they patiently waited this event, they might possibly have soon recovered

recovered all the common privileges of subjects. "For, adds my noble author, that gracious disposition in the King to his Catholic subjects, did not then appear ingrateful to any." But the vanity and presumption of some of them was great; they seized every opportunity of extolling their own loyalty; and they spoke of their sufferings in the Royal Cause as deserving of more than common notice. It is true, as I have already observed, they had done much. His Lordship even owns, that some of those, who had suffered most for his father, did send supplies to the King when he was abroad; "though, says he, they were hardly able to provide necessaries for themselves."

An address being made to the House of Peers, the year after the Restoration, for some relaxation of the laws against them, a committee of that house was appointed to examine and to report all those penal statutes, which reached to the taking away the life of any Catholic for his religion: "There not appearing one Lord in the house, who seemed to be unwilling that those laws should be repealed." After the committee was appointed, the Catholic Lords and
their

Charles II. their friends, for some days, diligently attended it, and made their observations on several acts of parliament, in which they desired ease. "But on a sudden this committee was discontinued, and never after revived; the Roman Catholics never afterwards being solicitous for it."

The truth is, they very soon quarrelled amongst themselves. The Lords and men of estates, little anxious about the abolition of laws, which concerned principally the lives of Priests, desired rather a repeal of those, whereby their own property, as Recusants, was affected. The churchmen, on the other hand, were not much solicitous about the removal of laws, by which sometimes they might gain the glory of martyrdom, whilst they continued under restraints more grievous far than death.—A committee was then chosen from among themselves of the superiors of all orders, and of the secular Clergy. They met at Arundell House, along with some of the principal Lords and Gentlemen. Here also dispute soon began, and they disagreed about the form of an oath or subscription, which it was intended should be made or taken by all Catholics.

Catholics. A proposition had likewise been made, that none but secular Priests should be tolerated in England, who should be under a Bishop and a settled form of government; and that all the regulars, in particular all Jesuits, should be, under the strictest penalties, forbidden the kingdom. The committee, as was natural to expect, was dissolved, and met no more.

From this time, owing to the imprudence of some, and the insolence of others, as also from that rooted dislike which the nation had not lost, Catholics again became common objects of aversion. They were regarded with an eye of peculiar jealousy from that known propension, which the King felt and ever expressed for them. Herein at least can be discovered no symptom of that ungrateful disposition, which, is said, so strongly to have marked the character of Charles. In his declaration for liberty of conscience to the Dissenters in 1662, he says, " It is divulged, through the kingdom, that we are highly indulgent to Papists, not only in exempting them from the penalties of the law, but even

Charles II. to such a degree of countenance and encouragement as may endanger the Protestant Religion.——It is true that, as we shall always, according to our justice, retain, so we think it may become us, to avow to the world the due sense we have, of the *greatest part* of our Catholic subjects of this kingdom, having deserved well of our royal father, of blessed memory, and from us, and *even from the Protestant Religion itself*, in adhering to us with their lives and fortunes, for the maintenance of our crown in the religion established, against those who, under the name of zealous Protestants, employed both fire and sword to overthrow them both.—Such are the capital laws in force against them, as that, though justified in their rigour by the times wherein they were made, we profess it would be grievous to us to consent to the execution of them, by putting any of our subjects to death for their opinion in matters of religion only.——But if, upon our expressing (according to Christian charity) our dislike of bloodshed for religion, and our gracious intentions to our Roman Catholic subjects, Priests shall take the boldness to appear, and avow themselves,

to

to the offence and scandal of good Protestants, and of the laws in force against them; they shall quickly find, we know as well to be severe, when wisdom requires it, as indulgent, when charity and sense of merit challenge it from us." This declaration, the most zealous Protestant must allow, is replete with good sense, and breathes that spirit of justice and love of order, which should ever animate the breasts of Princes: It also shews in what light the King considered the services he had received from his Catholic subjects.

In his speech to parliament, the year following, he again says, "The truth is, I am in my nature an enemy to all severity for religion and conscience, how mistaken soever it be, when it extends to capital and sanguinary punishments, which I am told began in Popish times. Therefore, when I say this, I hope I shall not need to warn any here, not to infer from thence, I mean to favour Popery. I must confess to you, there are many of that profession, who, having served my father, and myself very well, may fairly hope for some part of that indulgence, I

would

would willingly afford to others, who diffent from us. But let me explain myfelf, left fome miftake me herein, as I hear they did in my declaration. I am far from meaning by this a toleration, or qualifying them thereby to hold any offices or places in the government. Nay farther, I defire fome laws may be made to hinder the growth and progrefs of their doctrines."—In confequence of the laft claufe, a petition was prefented from both houfes that he would iffue a proclamation, commanding all Jefuits and Priefts to depart the kingdom by a day, under pain of having the penalties of the laws inflicted on them. To this the King confented.

The next year, 1664, a defign was formed, which came from the King himfelf, of bringing a bill into parliament, ferioufly meant to ferve the Catholics, by putting them on that footing of eafe and fecurity, which their conduct, as good fubjects, he thought merited. Meafures of afcertaining their numbers had been previoufly taken, that the moft violent might know there was nothing to be feared from fo inconfiderable a body. He
wifhed

wished also that a distinction should be made betwixt those, who, being of ancient extraction, had continued of the same religion from father to son, and those who became Proselytes to the Catholic Church. In the new bill it was intended to provide against such changes in religion. The King had likewise resolved to contract and lessen the number of Priests, and to reduce them into such order, that he might himself know all their names, and their several places of residence in the kingdom. " This measure, says Clarendon, must have produced such a security to those who stayed, and to those with whom they stayed, as would have set them free from any apprehension of any penalties imposed by preceding parliaments."—But this design, which comprehended many other particulars, from the perverse opposition of some weak heads of the party, vanished as soon as it was discovered. Moderate men, who desired nothing but the exercise of their religion in great secrecy, and a suspension of the laws, were cruelly disappointed, and in their conferences with the King often complained " of the folly and vanity of some of their friends, and more particularly

particularly of the presumption of the Jesuits." All further thoughts of the bill were now dropt, nor was there ever after mention of it.

From this view it may be justly inferred, that the Catholics at that time were their own greatest enemies. The King was decidedly their friend; the Courtiers, sunk in ease and luxury, laughed at all religion, and only wished to humour their Prince; the friends to Episcopacy and Monarchy, that is, the established Church, were not much inclined to oppose a party, who, they knew, would be ever ready to join them against the encroachments of the Sectaries; the Dissenters themselves, tho' enemies to the name of Catholic, now dared not speak out, whilst themselves were waiting redress from the crown; and the nation at large, just breathing from the horrors of civil commotions, wished not to be again exposed to the view of discord and contention. In such circumstances, nothing, it seems, could obstruct their prospects of success, but vain pretensions, immoderate confidence, precipitate counsels, imprudent zeal, or that animosity and internal discord, which must ever frustrate the best-concerted

certed plans. These were unfortunate evils; but they are the evils attendant on weak human nature: They were misfortunes which affected very sensibly the Catholic interest, but they had no immediate reference to the state. In allegiance, politics, and patriotism, the Catholics were steady, generous, and sincere.

In 1666, an event happened, which finally contributed to blast all their hopes, though Catholics were no otherwise concerned in it, than as sufferers, or as spectators sympathising in the general scene of misery and distress. The great fire of London was this event, and it was ascribed to the Papists. They had long acquired an exclusive claim to the infamy of every national calamity. Not the smallest proof of guilt was then adduced against them; but their crimes wanted not the useless formalities of proof. It was by some, however, given to Dutch or to French machinations, with equal semblance of truth. Clarendon, who was witness to the whole, ascribes it to the just judgment of Heaven, provoked by the general depravity of the nation. In common language, every moderate man considered it as accidental. But

Charles II. But the Magistracy of London, who are always wiser than the rest of mankind, saw into the whole transaction; and on a lying monument, raised where the fire began, with the greatest humanity ascribed it solely to the Papists. The noble pile to this day rears its head, an irrefragable argument of the blind credulity of the times!

The rumour of this calumny was but a prelude to many others, which easily found credit in a jealous and exasperated nation. A year now scarcely passed, in which some peculiar guilt was not imputed to Catholics. The public odium being again rouzed was easily kept alive; and the designs of bad men were answered. In 1670, the enemies to the court, who were greatly increased, publicly asserted that the King was now finally resolved to annul the constitution; that he aimed at arbitrary power, with a view of destroying the liberties of the people; and that he meant to subvert the established Church by an unlimited toleration of Popery. This was the magic wand, alone capable of realizing so momentous a design. The cabinet council, distinguished by the appellation

pellation of the *Cabal*, which Charles soon after chose, was indeed well calculated to give plausibility to these reports. They were not Catholics, (Clifford excepted) but they were the most dangerous Ministry that England perhaps ever knew. The Duke of York, with an imprudence that became his character, was, at the same time, far too open in declaring his religious sentiments. To give the last alarm to the fears of the nation, a formal liberty of conscience was allowed to all Sectaries. " This indulgence, says the King in his declaration, as to the allowance of public places of worship, and approbation of their Preachers, shall extend to all sorts of non-conformists and recusants, excepting to the recusants of the Roman Catholic religion; to whom we shall in nowise allow public places of worship, but only indulge them in their share in the common exemption from the execution of the penal laws, and the exercise of their worship in private houses only." Against this indulgence, in itself so just and reasonable, the parliament remonstrated, and the King was at last compelled to recal his declaration. Th

Charles II. unpopular conduct of the Ministry had raised a spirit of opposition, which would not be satisfied.

It is worth notice that, somewhat previous to the time I am speaking of, commenced the first secret money treaty between Louis XIV. and Charles; wherein it was stipulated that the latter should receive two hundred thousand pounds, for declaring himself a Catholic, and that France should assist him with troops, if his subjects rebelled. There were other articles of a nature equally singular. The destruction of Holland, in which England was to assist, was Louis's object. The Lords Clifford, and Arundel of Wardour, both Catholics, with Lord Arlington, a man well-affected to that religion, were appointed commissioners to transact this shameful business.—The year following, 1671, a similar treaty was concluded by Charles's Protestant Ministers, Buckingham, Ashley Cooper, and Lauderdale, who knew nothing of the first, excepting the article of the King's conversion, which, however, was secretly retained, this was a repetition of the former treaty.—Charles's views were only to get money; he was little solicitous about religion; and it is curious to see how artfully he afterwards evaded his promise of conversion.—These connexions with France were of the most fatal tendency, and the Royal Brothers, with all their Ministers, deserved to lose their heads.—From this time French money was largely distributed; and even the popular party, it is well known, entered into connexions with that nation, of a nature almost as dangerous as those which the Court is supposed to have formed against the religion and liberties of the subject.—Few parties in this kingdom are free from blame: In their turns, Whigs and Tories have been equally enemies to their country, when their passions and their interests misled them. "When I found, says Sir John Dalrymple, in the French dispatches, Lord Russell intriguing with the court of Versailles, and Algernon Sidney taking money from it, I felt very near the same shock, as if I had seen a son turn his back in the day of battle."—But to return.

Having gained this point, parliament proceeded further, and resolved to make

Charles II. the conformity in religious principles still more general. A law therefore passed, in 1673, intitled the *Test Act*, imposing an oath on all who should accept any public office. Besides the oaths of allegiance and supremacy, they were to receive the sacrament once a year in the established Church, and to abjure all belief in the doctrine of Transubstantiation. Peers were not included in this act; but if Papists, and held places by inheritance, they were obliged to appoint deputies.—The relation betwixt civil allegiance and a belief purely religious, is not, surely, very discoverable; but the object of this act was sufficiently obvious. It incapacitated every man from the service of his country, whose conscience should not be ductile enough to sacrifice his religion at the shrine of interest or of some paltry preferment.

The general disquietudes about religion did not however subside, and the people were instructed to consider the alliance, which had been made with France, as a fresh design for the introduction of Popery. The clouds began to thicken round the heads of Catholics. The nation was

was on tiptoe expecting some frightful event. Yet I cannot be prevailed on to think, it was at that unimportant body that were principally aimed the machinations of designing men. That same spirit, inimical to regal government, began again to move, which had for some time lain dormant, but had never been extinguished. In the breasts of others the horror of Popery was perhaps the sole actuating motive. But it was equally good policy in both to keep alive the popular apprehension. Charles would not depart from his favourite system of general moderation; it became therefore necessary to rouse him into action, and to this end the old stratagem of a *Plot* was thought the most efficacious measure. When the bad humours of Englishmen are once afloat, they must either have objects of suspicion on which to spend themselves, or they will make them.

The plot, which the infamous Mr. Titus Oates has honoured with his name, was broached in August, 1678. This man had discovered the secrets of a deep conspiracy, in which, it was represented, the Jesuits had a leading concern. They had

Charles II. had held several meetings, both abroad and in England, the final determination of which was to kill the King by poison, the gun, or a dagger. The glaring inconsistencies which crouded the narrative of this whole affair made no impression on a credulous public. It was their wish it might be true; and never was nation worked up to a higher pitch of foolish infatuation. Moderate men began to apprehend a general massacre of the whole Catholic body. Two events indeed accompanied the first opening of this plot, which contributed to give it some air of probability. These were the discovery of some letters of Coleman, Secretary to the Duke of York, and the death of Sir Edmondbury Godfrey. The letters were imprudent, and contained expressions about the introduction of Popery, which at this time were easily susceptible of further construction. The real truth is, Coleman was a weak and bigoted man, who wished to give a spread to his religion, but that only, as he declared on his trial, by procuring a free toleration for Catholics.—Godfrey's murder has never been cleared up; he was an active Justice of the Peace, and from a coincidence of his death with

the

the suppofed difcovery of the plot, the Papifts were charged with it. "There are feafons of believing, fays Burnet, as well as of difbelieving; and believing was then fo much in feafon, that improbabilities or inconfiftencies were little confidered. Nor was it fafe fo much as to make reflections on them. Oates, and Bedloe, another witnefs for the plot, continues the Bifhop, by their behaviour, detracted more from their own credit, than all their enemies could have done. The former talked of all perfons with an infufferable infolence; and the other was a fcandalous libertine in his whole deportment."

The King, from the beginning, was almoft the only perfon who treated the plot, as afcribed to Catholics, with becoming contempt. He faw through that dark veil, which the fafcinated multitude were unable to penetrate; whilft his Minifters ftood all aghaft, and either partook, or affected to partake of the general confternation. It was expected the parliament would reprefs thefe delufions, and would aim to call back the nation to reafon and deliberate enquiry. But they manifefted even greater credulity than the

the vulgar. The cry of *Plot* was echoed from one house to the other: The enemies to the crown would not let slip so favourable an opportunity of managing the passions of the people; and the court-party were afraid of being thought disloyal, should they seem to controvert the reality of the plot, or doubt the guilt of the pretended assassins of their King. " I would not, said a noble Lord, have so much as a Popish man or a Popish woman to remain amongst us, not so much as a Popish dog, or a Popish bitch, not so much as a Popish cat to mew, or pur about our King." This was sublime eloquence, and it was received with bursts of applause.—The Commons voted that the Papists designed to kill the King. Warrants were issued out, and many of that persuasion were apprehended. They were tried, convicted on the evidence of some of the worst men the earth ever bore, and executed. At death they still protested their innocence; a circumstance, says Mr. Hume, which made no impression on the spectators; their being Jesuits banished even pity from their sufferings. This frightful persecution continued for some time, and the King, contrary

trary to his own judgment, was obliged to give way to the popular fury.—"I waited often on him, says Burnet, all the month of December. He came to me to Chiffinch's, a page of the backstairs, and kept the time he assigned me to a minute. He was alone, and talked much, and very freely with me. We agreed in one thing, that the greatest part of the evidence was a contrivance. But he suspected some had set on Oates, and instructed him; and he named the Earl of Shaftesbury. I was of another mind. I thought the many grofs things in his narrative shewed, there was no abler head than Oates, or Tongue, in framing it: and Oates, in his first story, had covered the Duke, and the Ministers so much, that from thence it seemed clear that Lord Shaftesbury had no hand in it, who hated them much more than he did Popery. He fancied there was a design of rebellion on foot. I assured him, I saw no appearances of it. I told him, there was a report breaking out, that he intended to legitimate the Duke of Monmouth. He answered quick, that, as well as he loved him, he had rather see him hanged. Yet he apprehended a rebellion.

Charles II. bellion so much, that he seemed not ill pleased that the party should flatter themselves with that imagination, hoping that would keep them quiet in a dependence upon himself."—In the judgment of these two, it appears, how little the Catholics were concerned in this plot.

" It has been much doubted, says an author of great information, whether Shaftesbury contrived this plot, or if he only made use of it, after it broke out. Some papers I have seen convince me he contrived it, though the persons he made use of as informers ran beyond their instructions. The common objection to the supposition of his contriving the plot, is, the absurdity of its circumstances. When Shaftesbury himself was pressed with regard to that absurdity, he made an answer which shews equally the irregularity and the depth of his genius.—" It is no matter, said he, the more nonsensical the better; if we cannot bring them to swallow worse nonsense than that, we shall never do any good with them."

Catholic Peers were now excluded from sitting in the house, by a bill brought into

into parliament, requiring all members of either house, and all such as might come into the King's court, or presence, to take a test against Popery; in which not only Transubstantiation is renounced, but the invocation of the Virgin Mary and the Saints is declared to be idolatrous. This bill was principally levelled against the Duke of York; but he had interest enough to get himself excepted by a proviso annexed to it. Five of those Peers to whom the Pope, as Mr. Oates informed the public, had granted commissions to act as his ministers in England, had been sent to the Tower. Of these the Earl of Stafford, his Holiness's Paymaster-General, was alone executed; and at the death of this aged Nobleman the sternest countenances were seen to drop tears.

The new parliament of the succeeding year did not depart from the steps of their predecessors; and as the popular phrenzy seemed to abate, fresh means were devised for keeping up the alarm; mobs, petitions, and Pope-burnings were every day practised. The number of informing miscreants still encreased; the business was found to be not only lucrative, but honourable.

honourable. Plot was set up against plot, all of them under-parts of the same grand drama; and the minds of the nation were suspended in dreadful apprehension. This parliament also, to testify their loyalty, or to convince the world that they would not surrender the palm of infatuation, came to a resolution, " That if the King should come to any violent death, they will revenge it to the utmost on the Papists." A Papist only, in their judgment, had power to take away the life of a King! They did not probably recollect who had struck off the head of his late Majesty. The hand of every wretch was now armed with a dagger, by which he might at once destroy his Prince and extirpate Popery.

All this time Shaftesbury and his associates were labouring at their grand design; this was, to exclude the Duke of York from the throne, and to bring in the bastard Monmouth. The Duke was a Catholic: could it therefore be proved that the Papists with him at their head (for both he and the Queen were boldly accused of being accomplices in the plot) had conspired to kill the King, subvert the

the government, and bring in Popery, what further argument could be required for his exclusion and the utter extinction of his religion? The bill of exclusion was twice, with the most determined violence, brought into parliament; it passed the house of Commons, but the Lords threw it out by a great majority.

The King now became sullen and thoughtful; opposition had soured his temper, and he resolved to effect by resolution what mildness could not accomplish. The parliament spent their strength in vain efforts. During the recess, he had received the most adulatory addresses from his subjects; they censured the stubborn opposition of parliament, and offered to support the just rights of the crown. The popular commotions subsided, and the horrors of Popery seemed to wear away. The thinking part of the nation were seen to blush at their late wild credulity and extravagance: But an impression was made which no time will hardly efface. To the word *Popery*, before sufficiently tremendous in its sound, so many new ideas of terror were annexed, and so great ever since has been the aim of some men to maintain

maintain the delusion, that I am not surprised the minds of many should at this day feel its effects. Yet scarcely one person of common reading can be found, who does not acknowledge that the plot, I have described, was either the work of malice, or of design and faction.—In 1684 Charles died, and because, in his last moments, he professed himself a Catholic, it is probable that at all times, in his few serious hours, he had been strongly inclined to the principles of that religion.

The reader will be surprised, that I should have said nothing of a conspiracy, in which Protestants of the first distinction were concerned. The views of these men were various; the redress of grievances, the destruction of monarchy, or the gratification of revenge. These ends they aimed to obtain, by involving the kingdom in the horrors of a civil war; whilst underactors were, at the same time, engaged in a desperate scheme of assassinating the King and the Duke of York. These also were Protestants. The sword of sedition, with the bowl and dagger, were now taken into new hands; and had not Providence interfered, Charles, whose life had often been

been exposed to *imaginary* danger from the machinations of Papists, had *really* fallen by the authors of the Rye-House Plot. A writer, so disposed, might, on this occasion, recriminate with weighty retaliation; but my object is not to exculpate my own party, by a display of criminal excesses in their adversaries. I wish only *to speak of them as they were.* But if the pen of a Protestant can be excused from vicious partiality, who loads the whole Catholic body with opprobrious charges, for the follies in which a few were engaged; surely the same latitude may be allowed to others. It is a liberty, however, which the candid and honest historian will not be inclined to use.

Charles II.

THE death of Charles affected his subjects according to the different views of the parties, which then divided the nation. The Catholics were full of expectation from a Prince, who now openly professed their religion. The loyal Protestants, with law and the constitution on their side, had nothing, they thought, to apprehend, even from a Popish Monarch. The Whiggish faction alone had no favour to hope for; and

James II.

James II. and their late attempts had brought them into general difcredit with the nation. James the Second afcended the throne. Bigoted, headftrong, and imprudent, he had long, it feems, formed the defign of new-modelling the religion of his country. Had the exclufion-bill paffed, and James never reigned, it would have been well for Catholics. Yet the eafy fuppreffion of Monmouth's rebellion, and the execution of the heads of that defperate faction, feemed at firft to promife fuccefs to his moft fanguine fchemes. The barbarities committed by his officers on the defencelefs rebels, were, with much ill-nature, imputed to the King: It was faid, his religion delighted in blood. This was a wayward charge.—Very foon was exhibited a fcene of imprudences, which folly alone or treacherous defign could have dictated. James had admitted Catholic officers into his army, whom he difpenfed from the *Teft:* againft this the parliament remonftrated; he returned them a peevifh anfwer, and diffolved them. His determination then was to have a Catholic intereft in the Privy Council. Four Lords of that perfuafion were admitted; and the crafty Sunderland, with much piety declaring

ring himself a Papist, was nominated President. In other parts of the kingdom the old magistrates were displaced, and Catholics put in their room. Protestants very justly took the alarm, and the established Church, though ever loyal, shewed a face of determined opposition to such rash measures. A high Court of Ecclesiastical Commission was therefore appointed; and though wholly composed of Protestant members, it gave universal offence. Its office was to inspect all Church affairs; to reward the pliant, and to punish the refractory. It was a Court of *Inquisition*.— The next step was to grant liberty of conscience to all Sectaries. The King published his declaration, which contained much good sense, and great liberality of sentiment: But its drift was evident, and the nation loudly complained. Chapels were now opened, and the Catholic service publicly performed. Father Petre, a weak but designing Jesuit, appeared at Court, and was sometime after sworn a member of the Privy-Council. An Ambassador extraordinary was sent to Rome, to lay at his Holiness's feet the King's submission, and to solicit a mitre and a Cardinal's hat for the brows of Petre. The

James II. The Romans saw the folly of this precipitate conduct: "Your King, said they, should be excommunicated for thus attempting to overturn the small remains of Popery in England." A Nuncio was however sent, and he was received at Windsor with solemn pageantry.—He then attempted to obtrude his Catholic minions on the Universities: This was opposed with becoming resolution.—A second declaration for *liberty of conscience* was issued, with this particular injunction, that it should be read in all the Churches. The Bishops remonstrated; they were summoned before the Council; were sent to the Tower; were soon after tried—and acquitted.—The resentment of the people was now raised to the utmost: The King began to see the folly of his proceedings; he wished to call a parliament; and to effect that by constitutional means, which he had vainly attempted by every stretch of his dispensing power. It was now too late: News was brought him that William Prince of Orange was preparing a strong force to invade his territories. Dismayed and terrified, he now saw there was no redress, for he had forfeited all claim to the love of his subjects. The Prince landed; and
James

James forsook a throne which he was unfit, and, I think, unworthy, to govern.—When he first retired from London, the mob rose, and destroyed every Catholic Chapel in the city; nor was there a county in England, in which they did not leave some marks of their indignation.

Every attempt of James to subvert the established religion, or rather to give toleration to Catholics, (for this was all he then aimed at) was attended with the most glaring violations of the laws; and the powers he assumed of dispensing with them, without the consent of Parliament, broke asunder that sacred compact, by which the people are bound to their Sovereign. He was no longer entitled to their allegiance. Every patriot should have voted for his expulsion. Kings are made for the people, and the laws of the realm are their only rule of conduct: when they violate these, (it matters not under what pretence) they become tyrants.—It was unfortunate for James to have been so ill-advised. The inclinations of his own mind would not, I think, have hurried him on so far. But wicked and designing Ministers, leagued with weak and infatuated mes II. Priests, must at any time prove an overmatch for greater abilities than ever fell to the lot of a Stuart. The Catholics, as a body, merit not the reprehension, I give to Petre and his associates. They saw the wretched folly and the weak views of those bad advisers; and they condemned the precipitancy of measures which, they knew, could only terminate in their ruin. As must ever be the case with all men, in a similar situation, they wished to be relieved from oppression; but the undisturbed practice of their religion, with the enjoyment of some few civil liberties, would have satisfied their most sanguine desires. This I know from certain information: But unhappily for them and for their descendents, the voice of prudence and of cool religion was not attended to, whilst wild zeal and romantic piety were called in to suggest schemes of folly, and to precipitate their execution.

---

illiam III. AS the *Revolution*, in the year 1688, took place in opposition to James's wild projects of introducing Popery, the Catholics, it should seem, had much to apprehend from the event. But William was too good a politician to be inclined to ways of violence or persecution. He had been educated in a school, which taught him to appreciate merit or demerit in a subject, not from his religious tenets, but from the powers he possessed to promote or to oppose the designs of his master. Catholics therefore soon experienced the lenity of his government; and though the laws against them remained unrepealed, yet they were seldom put into rigorous execution. He considered them as a small member of the great Jacobitical body, whereof as the Protestants were, without comparison, the most formidable faction, his good sense told him that these were to be watched with peculiar jealousy. He also soon discovered, that tho' the Whigs had been principally instrumental in his elevation to the English throne, they were of a suspicious and untractable character, whose ideas of liberty were ever foremost, and who would never lose any opportunity of abridging the Royal Prerogative. The Catholics themselves were not dissatisfied with their condition; it was bad indeed, but they had expected it would have been much worse: And had not a false notion of Hereditary and Divine Right warped their judg-

judgments, and taught them to believe Loyalty to the house of Stuarts was a virtue of singular merit, they would probably have sat down, happy in the lowest condition of British subjects. But this was a preposseission not peculiar to Catholics; it had its votaries in every other religious persuasion.

In the beginning of his reign, to conciliate the affections of the Dissenters, whom he feared, the King passed the famous *Toleration Act*, by which they were freed from the penalties of the *Act of Uniformity*; and to indulge the ill humour of others, though contrary to his line of politics, yet, because he did not fear them, he permitted some severe statutes to be enacted against the Catholics. By these they are ordered to remove ten miles from Westminster; not to keep arms, or to be in possession of any horse above the value of five pounds; the Universities were vested with the advowsons belonging to them: and that the most distant hope of introducing Popery might be for ever precluded, an act of parliament passed declaring that no Papist, nor any one who marries a Papist, shall inherit the crown.

When

When James was in Ireland attempting to recover the sceptre he had forfeited, and when again, two years after, assisted by the French with a formidable fleet, he meditated a descent in England, the Catholics kept themselves quiet. I will not say, they did not wish him success, or that many would not have joined him, had he landed. Such measures their Jacobitism dictated, as it did to the rest of the party.—Nor, in the two desperate plots, which were formed to restore the fallen King, in the last of which the design was to assassinate William, are there any Catholics to be found of the least note or interest. Men of abandoned character and of desperate fortune, as I have often before observed, are always ready to engage in such attempts. But in both plots names were discovered of many Protestants, even of the Whiggish faction, which were capable of giving splendor to the darkest design. The King even wished not to know, says Burnet, the number of those who were in conspiracy against him, and declined all rigid enquiry.—It is rather singular, that factious men had now abandoned the old trick, of alarming the nation with the horrors of of some Popish plot, that their own schemes might go on unobserved: The reason probably was, they knew William to be a Prince too inquisitive to be imposed on by fiction; and too determined to be intimidated by the recital of imaginary dangers.

In 1699, the 11th of William, an act passed for *further preventing the growth of Popery*, of peculiar severity. A reward of a hundred pounds is offered for apprehending any Priest or Jesuit: Papists not taking the oaths in six months, after eighteen years of age, are declared incapable to inherit lands, &c. and the next of kin, a Protestant, to enjoy the same; also Papists are made incapable to purchase lands: Ambassadors not to protect Priests that are subjects of England: a hundred pounds forfeit for sending a child to be educated abroad in the Romish Religion: Popish parents obliged to allow a maintenance to their children, becoming Protestants, at the Chancellor's determination.—The last clause excepted, there is something so singularly cruel in this act, made at a time when it does not appear that Catholics had given any just cause of provocation, that

that to a person, unacquainted with the circumstances in which it passed, it must appear strangely unaccountable. This is the act, parts of which the humanity and Christian moderation of a British Parliament has lately thought proper to repeal.——I shall give in Bishop Burnet's own words, who was at the time himself in the house, a short history of the passing of this singular act.

"Upon the peace of Ryswick, says he, (two years before) a great swarm of Priests came over to England, not only those whom the Revolution had frightened away, but many more new men, who appeared in many places with great insolence; and it was said, that they boasted of the favour and protection of which they were assured. Some enemies of the government began to give it out, that the favouring of that religion, was a secret article of the peace; and so absurd is malice and calumny, that the Jacobites began to say, that the King was either of that religion, or at least a favourer of it: Complaints of the avowed practices and insolence of the Priests were brought from several places, during the last Session of Parliament, and those were
maliciously

maliciously aggravated by some who cast the blame of all on the King.

"Upon this, some proposed a bill, that obliged all persons educated in that religion, or suspected to be of it, who should succeed to any estate before they were of the age of eighteen, to take the oaths of Allegiance and Supremacy, and the Test, as soon as they came to that age; and till they did it, the estate was to devolve to the next of kin, that was a Protestant; but was to return back to them, upon their taking the oaths. All Popish Priests were also banished by the bill, and were adjudged to perpetual imprisonment, if they should again return to England; and the reward of a hundred pounds was offered to every one who should discover a Popish Priest, so as to convict him. Those who brought this into the House of Commons, hoped that the Court would haved opposed it; but the Court promoted the bill; so when the party saw their mistake, they seemed willing to let the bill fall; and when that could not be done, they clogged it with many severe and some unreasonable clauses, hoping that the Lords would not pass the act; and
it

it was said, that if the Lords should make William
the least alteration in it, they, in the house
of Commons, who had set it on, were resolved to let it lie on their table, when it
should be sent back to them. Many Lords,
who secretly favoured Papists, on the Jacobite account, did, for this reason, move
for several alterations; some of these im-
porting a greater severity; but the zeal
against Popery was such in that house, that
the bill passed without any amendment,
and it had the Royal Assent."

DURING the thirteen years of Queen Anne.
Anne's reign, who, on the death of William
in 1702, succeeded to the throne, Catholics were permitted to live free from molestation, subject only to such restraints as
former laws had imposed. They were by
no means disagreeable to Anne; she recol-
lected the loyalty they had alway shewn
to her family; nor did their present attachment to her unfortunate brother James
give her displeasure. Her throne was too
firmly fixed to be shaken by a reed so
broken.—The profession of the same political opinions with the Tories, contributed
not a little to procure them some ease in

L. From

Anne. from that powerful faction; it removed part of the odium that had been annexed to the name of Papist.—The Whigs continued to detest them, not now so much from hatred of their religion, as because their Tory principles threw some weight into the scale of their opponents.—The nation at large, amused with the sound of victories, which on all sides attended our arms, and engaged in the animosity of political altercations, lost sight of every other object: Enthusiasm in politics had taken place of Enthusiasm in religion.—The leading men of the Catholic party, though removed from the concerns of state, warmly espoused the Tory interest; whilst the body itself, now reposing from the violence of former oppression, seemed to enjoy their present small allotment of ease, and sometimes perhaps amused themselves with the vain reflection, that at the death of Anne, their favourite James might be called to the throne of his ancestors. In their turn they hated the Whigs, whom they considered as the instruments of the Revolution; and though this event had proved the real cause of their present happiness, it would have been criminal, they thought, to have indulged any favourable emotions towards

towards them. Such was the character of their loyalty; and at that time a Whig-Catholic would have been deemed a phenomenon, fit only to excite the detestation of some, and the amazement of others.

At the end of the session in 1706, great complaints were made in both houses of parliament of the growth of Popery, particularly in Lancashire, and of great imprudencies committed both by the Laity and Priests of that communion. I do not find what these imprudencies were. A bill was therefore brought into the Lower House, with such clauses, as would have rendered more effectual the late act of King William. The Catholics made powerful intercession. The court seemed indifferent in the matter; whilst the enemies to the bill represented it as unreasonably severe at a time, when we were in alliance with so many Princes of that religion, and when the Queen was actually interceding for indulgence to the Protestants in their dominions. It was contrary also, they said, to those maxims of liberty of conscience and toleration, which now began so generally to prevail.—It was answered, that the avowed dependence

Anne. of Papists on a foreign jurisdiction, and at present on a foreign Pretender to the crown, put them in a situation widely different from that of other Dissenters; that they were rather to be considered as enemies to the state, than as British subjects.—The first of these charges was a groundless accusation, the second was equally applicable to the whole Jacobitical Faction.—The bill dropt; and an address was made to the Queen that she would order a return, of all the Papists in England, to be prepared, for the next session of parliament.

The violent commotions, which were raised in 1709, on account of the doctrine of Non-resistance and other Tory-maxims, advanced in a sermon by Sacheverel, though partly of a religious complexion, contributed not a little to draw the attention of the public from all considerations of Popery. The established Church warmly espoused his cause, declaring their abhorrence of all Whiggish doctrines; and the popular fury, which before had always raged against Popery, flamed out with unusual violence against the Dissenting Protestants. The cry was, *The Church and*

and Sacheverel. In their madness, they destroyed several Meeting-Houses, plundered the dwellings of many eminent Dissenters, and even, it is said, proposed to attack the Bank itself. Some people of better fashion were supposed to direct these proceedings; they followed the mob in hackney coaches, and were seen sending messages to them. At this time, a Catholic, with Sacheverel's sermon in his hand, might have preached all the doctrines of Rome at Charing Cross, and have received the shouts of the multitude: So small were the remains of common reason and consistent sense!

In the twelfth year of her Majesty, some other complaints being made against Catholics, though I cannot find of what nature they were, a bill passed against them, for rendering more effectual the act of King William. By this they are disabled from presenting to benefices; and the benefices in their presentation are confirmed to the two Universities, who may prefer bills in Chancery to discover fraudulent trusts.

PUR-

George I. PURSUANT to the *Act of Succession*, on the death of Anne, George the First, the next Protestant heir, came to the throne in 1714.—The friends to James now saw all their schemes for his restoration at once blasted, and themselves exposed to the frowns of their new King. The exultation of the Whigs was indeed unbounded, when the road to honours and exclusive favour lay open before them, and their enemies were fallen at their feet. George could not but view those men in a favourable light, who had so long professed themselves his friends, and to whose exertions he owed his crown. The Tories were his enemies, and they expected little favour. As to the Catholics, though it was well known they would have bled to impede his succession, yet the King was only disposed to view them in the common light of other opponents. In Germany he had learned a lesson of religious moderation. Where Catholics and Protestants blend promiscuously together, and pray to God under the same roof, all acirmony and marks of odious distinction must necessarily disappear. He likewise perceived, they were too insignificant to create any uneasy solicitude; nor did he wish to provoke a worm by wanton severities. The word *Popery* to his ears conveyed no ideas of horror: *Jacobitism* was a sound more replete with danger and suspicion. The Catholics themselves, though sorely disappointed, were little inclined to murmur, when they saw before them a fair prospect of tranquillity, which nothing, it appeared, but their own folly could disturb. They were therefore easy under this new arrangement; those only excepted, whose dreams of loyalty, disturbing the obvious suggestions of prudence and common sense, rendered unsatisfied and restless. But as yet no occasion offered for exertion. With others of the same description, they therefore sat down, in sullen resignation, brooding over their airy prospects of golden days, framing plans of vast execution, and cherishing, in great self-complacency, all the comforts of those exalted virtues, which Jacobitism only could inspire.

The popular cry against the Dissenters still prevailing, they were branded as the promoters of opinions, from which not only heterodoxy, but vice of every kind, were daily gaining strength. The established Church, it was said, stood in imminent

George I. imminent danger of subversion. The Clergy were loud in their complaints; but they were now silenced, and all disputations on religious topics were prohibited. But these methods proving inefficacious to stop the mouth of opposition, an artifice of singular power was devised. *Jacobitism* and *Popery* were made synonymous terms; and all such as testified any discontent against government were branded with the double appellation. The Tories were universally involved in this imputation; whilst the real Catholics, besides the old stigma of their religion, had also to bear the charge of political heterodoxy. The Whigs triumphed in this fortunate stratagem: It sunk the popularity of their opponents; nor could the effect be evaded, since it was well known that the charge in general was founded on truth. The Tories were, in principle at least, friends to Jacobitism, and so were the Papists; they should not therefore, it seemed, be great enemies to each other. From this time, and for many years to come, the words *Jacobite* and *Papist* remained inseparably united.

In the rebellion of 1715, so rashly concerted to restore the Pretender, we find names of every description in religion and politics; Tories, Whigs, Church of England-Men, Dissenters, and Catholics. The discontented of all parties engaged. It can be no surprise, if many Catholics espoused the wild attempt: Their attachment to James, as I have said, was of the most sincere and sanguine character; and the religious prejudices of many at that time were warm enough to inspire them with enthusiasm in the cause. The number of real insurgents was, however, inconsiderable: The whole body wished him success, but the ardour of all was not sufficiently flaming to lead them to the field of action.—The forfeiture of property, which succeeded the execution of some of the principal Catholic rebels, was a great blow to the interest of the body; but fortunately the blood then spilt read a lesson to the rest of the party, which has proved highly useful to their posterity. From that day, their loyalty began to cool, and Jacobitism was little more than an empty sound.

When men act from principles, however erroneous, they acquire a consistency of character, which, by proper management, may be directed to much good. George weighed attentively the motives, which had drawn the Catholics into the late rebellion; he admired their steady, though mistaken loyalty; he pitied their blindness; and he wished to reclaim them. A project therefore, in the year 1719, was set on foot, and I believe with serious design, to give them ease, and thereby to ensure their future allegiance. Ministry were engaged in the scheme, and seemed to wish it success. But this also ended just as every other project had ended before. The committee of Catholics, appointed to conduct the business, disagreed amongst themselves; the affair sunk, and was heard of no more. The principal agent was Dr. Strickland, afterwards Bishop of Namur, who was very intimate with the King, and whose views, had they been followed, might have brought certain relief to his party. But there was a narrowness in the minds of Catholics, Laity as well as Clergy, which little less than miraculous powers could have enlarged. Thanks to Heaven! those powers, from that time, began to operate, and the present generation dares to think and to act, on a more liberal and extensive plan.

Some laws, even during this reign, were made against Catholics. Their hard fate would have it, that no era of British History should be left without some mark of their oppression! By the first of George, within six months after they come to the age of twenty-one, they are obliged to register their names and estates with the clerk of the peace: The non-compliance with this form to be punished with forfeiture of estate, &c.—By the third of George, they are charged with an additional expence in every family-transaction, by being compelled to inroll all deeds, &c.——They are also loaded with the payment of a double sum affixed upon Protestants by the land-tax act; but this, I believe, was first ordered in the reign of William.

———————————

THE thirty-three years of George the second's reign, which began in 1727, exhibit no material change in the condition of Catholics. They continue in the same state of tranquillity, unengaged spectators of those turbulent scenes, in which the nations of Europe were successively occupied. One event only happened, which I shall presently notice, in which they were concerned, and which probably, if human foresight may be allowed to judge, will be the last.

From the ease they had now, for a long time, enjoyed, and which, compared with their former state of perpetual vexation, was very great, Catholics had become more sociable; they began to taste those sweets of life, which liberty and open intercourse with the world can supply. As the weight of oppression lightened, and the severity of penal prosecution ceased, the stern vigour of their minds relaxed, and they every day lost something of that enthusiasm of soul, which the sufferers for real, or for fancied justice, always experience. Such enthusiasm can give charms to oppression or to death. The consequences of this change were evident. Men of family grew daily less zealous in religion; their wonted loyalty abated; and they insensibly reformed first their politics, and soon after often conformed

to

to the established Church. Already, during the present century, this has been the case with many; and every year will now continue to witness the progress of the same revolution. The splendor of the party by such means vanished; whilst the remaining multitude were viewed as an object, capable of raising, nor love, nor hatred, nor envy, nor suspicion: and had not the late rebellion of 1745 unfortunately intervened, before this day, probably, the name of Popery would have been an unheeded sound, and all execution of the penal statutes utterly suspended.

At the instigation of French counsels, who never meant to give him any real support, and hurried on by the bad advice of his misjudging friends, and his own vain ambition, the young Pretender, with an army of seven men, landed in Scotland. In this Northern soil, so congenial with its nature, had long been planted the tree of rebellion, and under its deadly shade grew many noxious herbs, favourable to the nurture of bigotry, fanaticism, treason, and all the selfish and unsociable passions. The Scots often resorted to this fatal spot, and in large draughts

George II. draughts drank down the contagion; here they met the young adventurer. The first fuccefs, and fubfequent events, of this rafh invafion are well known. Its chief, and almoft only, fupport was from Scotland, affifted afterwards by a few Englifh, and of thefe a very fmall part were Catholics. There appeared no real difpofition in the reft of the party to join him, though their wifhes were very fervent for his fuccefs. A general alarm was now given to the nation, and the old cry of *Popery* was echoed from fhore to fhore. The rebellion, however, was foon terminated. Some lives were forfeited, and the tumults fubfided. But a frefh impreffion was again made, which called up the former animofity of the nation, and it was faid by many, that Papifts would never peaceably fubmit to a Proteftant government. This was an ill-natured charge. For very few Catholics, I have obferved, were engaged in the rebellion: and if the body muft fuffer for the follies of thefe few, furely the fame fhould be the fate of Proteftants; for of thefe, fome in England, and many in Scotland, joined the Rebel ftandard. There is alfo fomething to plead in favour of Catholics, which is

not

not applicable to Proteſtants. Theſe men enjoyed all the privileges of Britiſh ſubjects, whilſt the former were oppreſſed; and this for the original ſin imputed to their anceſtors, in which they at leaſt had no concern. When a proſpect of relief opens, may not the wretched ſtrive to enter? But he that is not eaſy on a bed of roſes, deſerves to be laid on thorns.

George II.

When the popular fury had ſubſided on the extinction of the rebellion, the Catholics gradually returned to their ſtate of tranquillity; and thus they lived, peaceable and unoffending ſubjects, complying with the reſpective duties of civil life, and worſhipping God in the very retired and ſecret manner, the lenity of government allowed, during the remaining part of his Majeſty's reign.

In the ſhort view, I have exhibited, the reader has ſeen the ſucceſſive revolutions and changes to which the Catholics of England have been ſubjected from the Reformation, almoſt down to the preſent day. It is unneceſſary to recapitulate events, where the ſubject has been drawn to ſo ſmall a point. I have him therefore

George II. to his own reflections. One observation only I wish to add; that in no part of the history of mankind do we meet with any society, who have made fewer attempts to regain their lost privileges, or who for these attempts have been subjected to severer penalties. In their constant behaviour to Catholics, I can no where discover the least trace of that liberal, humane, and manly spirit which, on every other occasion, is seen to animate the breasts of Englishmen. Yet we are the old stock, from whence they sprung.

George III. NO occurrence, of sufficient weight to call the historian's attention, having happened in the concerns of Catholics, for the seventeen first years of his Majesty's reign, I hasten to the transactions of 1778, when a bill was obtained, by which some relief was granted them from the severity of a former statute. The uniform tenour of their conduct, in circumstances of real trial, had convinced their greatest enemies, that now at least they deserved the indulgence of government. If they may not enjoy unlimited toleration, said they, we
should

should not, however, oppress unoffending citizens.

A Philosopher, who should have viewed the general features of the nation, at this time, would have been induced to believe, that a more favourable opportunity never could have offered, for an oppressed party to sue for redress. The bigotry and narrow fancies of former days seemed melted down into extensive philanthropy, and a mild indulgence even to the errors of our fellow-creatures. In Church, the great points of religious toleration had been ably investigated; and very few there were, on the bench of Bishops, who were not strongly disposed to allow the fullest liberty to Dissenters of every description.—State politicians concerned themselves little in affairs of conscience; they had objects of another nature to attend to, which demanded more than common exertion; besides, they wished the concurrence of all men to their schemes, whether of war or of peace.—The enemies to government were numerous and determined; but they were men peculiarly liberal in sentiment, and whose notions of extensive freedom could not surely be reconciled with the smallest

smallest element of oppression.———The higher ranks in life affected to think lightly of religion in general: To them every species of persecution was an absurdity, odious and contemptible. Many of them had travelled, and had seen religion in all its modes; they had dined with Cardinals, and perhaps conversed with the Pope; and had found him to be a good-tempered, inoffensive old man, without either horns or cloven feet.—The multitude, as is ever the case, copied their superiors: Much irreligion every where prevailed amongst them, particularly in the towns; it was not therefore to be apprehended, they would be alarmed with any indulgence allowed to Catholics.—The Disciples of Wesley only, and some of the Dissenting congregations, appeared to retain the illiberal stiffness of old times; the word *Popery* to their ears was still a sound of horror. But then the Dissenters were themselves petitioning for relief, and the Methodists, it was hoped, had not totally lost the mild character of the established Church, of which they still affect to be members.—At the head of all, George the Third was known to have inherited the religious moderation of his family; and

in

in him this amiable disposition had been early improved by a philosophic and liberal education. He knew, the Catholics of England were good subjects; he knew, the old popular cry against Popery, though for one time politically kept up to serve his family, was at this day disingenuous and sordid; and he knew, that the attachment they had to the Stuarts, was now universally transfered to the house of Hanover. In that steadiness of mistaken loyalty so long preserved, he discovered a sure pledge of the unalterable permanency of their present allegiance.—In this state of things the Catholics were advised first to address his Majesty, and then to petition parliament for relief. The success, which attended these measures, convinced them, that they were not deceived in the favourable notions they had formed of the times. It has been said that the Popish bill was *insidiously* brought into parliament at the end of a session, when many of the members were out of town, and when the others wished to retire. It has also been said; that had time been allowed for cool reflection, or had the sense of the nation been maturely taken, the bill had never passed.—The *fact*, with regard to the

the firſt allegation, is true. But it ſo happened by no intentional or colluſive deſign. The Catholics themſelves, as I well know, never thought of petitioning for relief till towards the end of Lent of that year, and from that time there was not a day to loſe. This, I believe, was rather a fortunate circumſtance. For though no bill could have paſſed with more concurrent approbation of both houſes, which were by no means thin, as is falſly aſſerted; yet had leiſure been given for the ill humour of bigotry and of Scotch fanaticiſm to ferment, moſt probably, to judge from late experience, an oppoſition might have been blown up, far too powerful for all the efforts of good ſenſe and Chriſtian moderation. But the nation at large was not diſpleaſed with the bill. Their ſenſe is to be taken, whilſt they are cool and temperate; and not when ſedition has raiſed diſcontents and murmurs, by the bad arts of miſrepreſentation and calumny. This was moſt notoriouſly practiſed: For when parliament lately examined the grounds, from which roſe the popular clamour, it was found that no ſingle charge, urged by the petitioning Proteſtants, was true. The Catholics

Catholics had taken no unfair advantage of the indulgence granted them; they had opened no new Schools; had built no additional Chapels; had inveigled no Proteſtant children; had laboured to make no new Proſelytes; in a word, they had lived in the ſame retired, unoffending manner, as had been, for many years, their wonted practice. Their countenances had perhaps put on a more cheerful air, and did Engliſhmen envy them this portion of happineſs!

The indulgence they had obtained, tho' they were thankful for it, was after all but a ſmall favour. The new bill repealed only ſome parts of the act of the 12th of King William; thoſe which related to the apprehending of Popiſh Biſhops and Prieſts, and ſubjected them, as alſo Papiſts keeping ſchool, to perpetual impriſonment; likewiſe that clauſe which diſabled Catholics from inheriting or purchaſing lands. But they were not to benefit even of this indulgence, unleſs, within a limited time, they took and ſubſcribed an oath, in itſelf ſufficiently humiliating, which was prepared for them.—The other clauſes of this act, with the whole code of other ſevere

severe and sanguinary laws, remained, and do now remain, in full force against them. Yet the public has been told, that an unlimited Toleration had been granted to Catholics. Were the authors of such malignant reports reduced to their state, the slaves in the plantations of Jamaica would have little reason to envy their condition. The act of William, from the reward it held out to informers, of which bad use had often been made, and from the particular circumstances which attended its original formation, was judged to be peculiarly deserving of this partial repeal.

I am not disposed to enter into a detail of those riotous proceedings, which disgraced the month of June of 1780; they are still fresh in every one's memory; and they will continue to blacken the annals of English history to the latest times.— I have before me an accurate narrative of the transactions of each meeting of the Protestant Association, previous to their fatal assembly in St. George's Fields. It was taken by a person, who gave painful attendance at their several convocations. Neither reason, humanity, nor religion, were ever permitted to enter their doors; wild

wild uproar, ranting declamation, and low calumny, directed their councils, and dictated their resolves. The event answered such antichristian deliberations.——The scheme of opposition, taken up by these mad reformers, originated in Scotland. They had set the example; and they gave them a President well adapted to the work. The Scots gloried, that by so nobly withstanding every design to give relief to their Catholic fellow-subjects at home, they had fought the battles of the Lord, and had triumphed. They were ready, they said, to march into England, to prosecute the holy war, and to sacrifice to the manes of Knox, those friends to superstition and idolatry, who had dared to listen to the soft suggestions of humanity and reason, rather than to the howls of intolerant fanaticism.—The reader will excuse my warmth when I speak of these men: It is Philosophy pleading the cause of human nature in the year 1780.—I must add, if Ministry had acted with becoming fortitude in the riots of Scotland, we should not probably have seen a Protestant Association in London. But firmness is not a virtue of modern growth.

George III. With pleasure I could draw a contrast betwixt the behaviour of Catholics and that of their enemies. Whilst these were meditating schemes of oppression and cruelty, they silently looked on; nor could they be persuaded to think that any application to parliament, for a repeal of their bill, was seriously intended. Conscious of the rectitude of their own conduct, they wished not to impute such bad designs to any men. Otherwise a timely application might probably have frustrated the projected plan. When the riots began, their behaviour was still more exemplary. With pain they viewed themselves as the innocent occasion of such wild and calamitous tumults; and they lamented to see soldiers marching into London, those dangerous protectors of the lives and property of British citizens. They could have themselves repelled the most determined attacks of that lawless rabble; and it was with difficulty that a brave insulted band of Irish Catholics were restrained from dreadful retaliation. At one time, the innate principle of self-preservation seemed to call for such a measure. But fearful of adding to the scene of consternation, and desirous of convincing their greatest enemies,

mies, that the love of order and of peace was, in their minds, superior to all other considerations, the Catholics rather chose to see their property destroyed, and themselves shamefully insulted, than to resist. The principles of such men are not surely of that dark complexion, which misrepresentation has instructed the mind of ignorance to believe. Their only wish had been, to possess their own property in legal security, to educate their own children, and to worship God in the manner their consciences directed. This privilege the laws of nature seem to allow to all men; but when a British Parliament had granted it to Catholics, a mob of British Protestants tumultuously demanded its revocation.

George III.

It is time to lose sight of this horrid transaction, and coolly to pursue another object. Reflection naturally occurs to every man, and if himself uninformed, he wishes to ask the following question: " Is there really any thing in the manners or in the principles of Catholics, at the present day, that can justly give alarm to government, as now established in Church or State?" It matters not, what all or any

Conclusion.

Conclusion. of that body may have thought or practised in former times; nor does it regard us, what may now be the sentiments of Catholics in other countries. We wish information with regard to those few only, who actually live amongst us. The clamours of a mob, or the declamatory discourses of ignorant, selfish, and bigoted men, deserve no attention; they must ever deceive us: but in cool and dispassionate temper, we desire to receive such instructions, as can only be supplied by those, who are themselves Catholics, and who are thoroughly acquainted with the real state of that body now in England.

The author of these sheets flatters himself, he can give this information: he was educated in an English College abroad; he has since that lived and conversed with people of all ranks in that persuasion at home: he is himself a Catholic, and has long made the study of their principles a serious occupation; and, from what has already been delivered in the foregoing pages, he presumes, his readers will not think him too much biassed to his own party, or improperly warm in his representation of men and things. He trusts also, that his

his Catholic friends will not be offended at the candid description he is going to exhibit of their manners, principles, state, and circumstances. If the view prove sometimes unpleasant, he is not blameable. The artist who sits down to draw a landscape, must, with equal fidelity, describe the dreary wilderness and the flowery plain, if they be real parts of the scene before him.

Conclusion.

END *of the* FIRST PART.

A VIEW of ENGLISH CATHOLICS, LAITY and CLERGY;

THEIR

NUMBER, WEALTH, CHARACTER, &c.

In the PRESENT YEAR, 1780.

PART II.

IT is surely inconsistent with the character of a great nation to be intimidated by imaginary apprehensions; yet it often happens that greater alarms are raised by such impressions, than by the approach of real and weighty danger. We have seen how astonishingly this kingdom has been repeatedly convulsed by fictitious plots and the vain dread of Popery. The event has always proved that such fear was causeless.——Another misfortune is, that most men, either from indolence or from

Introduct

Introduction from want of opportunities, take their information from the report of others; little reflecting, that they who are most ready to inform, are frequently actuated by motives widely distant from the love of truth. To receive such instructions without further enquiry, argues a rash, weak, or a malevolent heart.—When a nation, in any branch of its establishment, is in danger from the supposed designs of a party, there must be something in the principles or in the circumstances of the latter, on which suspicions may be founded. The politician will then take a circumscriptive view. From whatever quarter he is instructed to look for danger, that way he will direct his sight. He has learned, from perusing the history of mankind, that the powers of any faction to do mischief are, in a well-regulated state, extremely limited; and he has also learned that such powers are generally exerted in a similar manner. Human nature is the same in all its evolutions. He has therefore a clue given him, whereby his researches may be drawn to a sure conclusion. If Catholics be a faction dangerous to the state, they must be so in the manner of other factions: The point will be easily

easily decided; for they are not surely endowed with powers of preternatural energy.

AFTER repeated enquiries, I am not yet able to ascertain the real number of Catholics. I have seen some computations, which are said to have been made, but they are all exaggerated past belief. From the best information, I can procure, their number does not, at this day, exceed 60,000: and this even, I suspect to be far beyond the mark.—If the Bishops go on with their scheme, parliament will soon be in possession of returns, which must be considered as accurate and authentic. But I wish them to be more carefully attentive than others have been, who formerly undertook the work. Dr. Blackburne, I think, a few years back, made out an account from a certain district in the north, with which he is well-acquainted, which was shamefully false.—Men violently prejudiced, like some insects, see with polyhedron optics; that is, their eyes multiply. Solicitous to make Catholics appear an object of terror, because in their cradles they were often frightened with the name, they chuse to avoid all accurate computation.—

London excepted, very little difficulty would attend a moſt exact *cenſus*. It has not hitherto been done from indolence or inattention: yet I much wiſh, for reaſons to me very obvious, that ſome Catholic would at this moment undertake it. In London there would be great difficulty: but a third part at leaſt of their number in that town are foreigners. A watchful government would thin this motley crew, and ſend them back to their own countries. Their only aim is to emaſculate the genuine character of Engliſhmen, or to eat a bread deſigned for better induſtry.

When we take a view of the great body of the nation, on the moderate computation of ſix millions, even the exaggerated numbers of Catholics vaniſh to an imperceptible point. Some of the great trading and manufacturing provincial towns are known to contain more inhabitants, than our whole collective numbers amount to. Briſtol would think itſelf ſadly depopulated, if reduced to ſixty thouſand ſouls. Yet the public is taught to believe that the Britiſh conſtitution is in danger from the attempts of this inſignificant multitude! The army they could bring into the

[113]

the field, though preceded by the Pope's banner, and fortified with his holy benediction, would cause little terror, I fancy, on the day of action, to the *heretical* force of England. In reading the adventures of Don Quixote, we laugh at the folly of a man, who at every turn could raise up to himself imaginary foes: The conduct of those, who speak gravely of the terrifying numbers of Catholics, is not less ridiculous.*

P   The

---

* "While King William was engaged in his project of reconciling the religious differences of England, he was at great pains to find out the proportions between Churchmen, Dissenters, and Papists. In his Cabinet there is the following curious report in consequence of an enquiry upon that head.

The number of FREEHOLDERS in ENGLAND.

	Conformists	Nonconformists	Papists
Province of Canterbury	2,123,362	93,151	11,878
of York	353,892	15,525	1,978
In both	2,477,254	108,676	13,856
Conformists	2,477,254		
Non-conformists	108,676		
	2,585,930		
Papists	13,856		
In all England	2,599,786		

"In the Province of Canterbury are 23,740 Papists, half of these are under the age of sixteen years, viz. 11,870; a seventh part of these are aged, and above 3,391. The king

The few Catholics, I have mentioned, are also dispersed in the different counties. In many, particularly in the West, in South-Wales, and in some of the midland counties, there is scarcely a Catholic to be found. This is easily known from the residence of Priests. After London, by far the greatest number is in Lancashire. In Staffordshire are a good many, as also in the northern counties of York, Durham, and Northumberland. Some of the manufacturing and trading towns, as Norwich, Manchester, Liverpool, Wolverhampton,

king out of the said number of Papists the two last sums, which make in all 15,201; there remains then 8,478, of which the one half are women: there remains therefore in the Province of Canterbury, fit to bear arms, 4,239 Papists.

"The Province of York bears a sixth part of the taxes, and has in it a sixth part of the people as that of Canterbury has, viz. 3,050, whereof half are under the age of sixteen, viz. 1,525, and a seventh part above sixty, viz. 565; and of the aforesaid sixth part one half is women.—The total therefore of this Province fit to bear arms is 701; joining which to the total of those in the Province of Canterbury fit to bear arms, makes the total of the Papists throughout all England fit to bear arms to be 4,940."

I have taken this from the appendix to Sir John Dalrymple's Mem­. I cannot think it is by any means accurate: It seems to diminish the number of Catholics as much as later returns augment it. Should it be true, we have greatly increased since that time; whereas I certainly know we are much diminished within this century.

hampton, and Newcastle-upon-Tyne, have Chapels, which are rather crowded, but these constitute the greatest part of the number I have just given to their respective counties. In a few towns, particularly at Coventry, their number, I find, is increased; but this by no means in proportion of the general increase of population in the same places. Excepting in the towns, and out of Lancashire, the chief situation of Catholics is in the neighbourhood of the old families of that persuasion. They are the servants, or the children of servants, who have married from those families, and who chuse to remain round the old mansion, for the conveniency of prayers, and because they hope to receive favour and assistance from their former masters.

Many laws have been enacted to prevent the growth of Popery; and it now is, and always has been, the popular cry, that Papists are daily increasing. One might almost fancy, from the frequency of these reports, that they sprang up, like mushrooms, by spontaneous vegetation. Had there been truth in such reports, how very different, at this day, would be the list of

P 2   Catholic

Catholic names, from what it really is. More than one half, if not the whole English nation, must have been long ago subjected to the See of Rome. The truth is, within the present century we have most rapidly decreased. Many congregations have intirely disappeared in different parts; and in one district alone, with which I am acquainted, eight out of thirteen are come to nothing; nor have any new ones risen to make up, in any proportion, their loss. These are facts of certain notoriety.—In the nature of things, it could not possibly be otherwise. Where one cause can be discovered tending to their increase, their will be twenty found to work their diminution. Among these the principal are, the loss of families by death, or by conforming to the established Church; the marrying with Protestants; and that general indifference about religion, which gains so perceptibly on all ranks of Christians.—When a family of distinction fails, as there seldom continues any conveniency either for prayers or instruction, the neighbouring Catholics soon fall away: And when a Priest is still maintained, the example of the Lord is wanting to encourage the lower class, particularly

to

to the practice of their religion. I recollect the names of at least ten noble families that, within these sixty years, have either conformed, or are extinct; besides many Commoners of distinction and fortune.—The marrying with Protestants, which is now very usual, will necessarily produce the same effect. All, or half the children are, in this case, generally educated Protestants; and when this is not done, example or persuasion often proves equally efficacious.—I need not insist on the operation of the third cause I mentioned.—When we add to these the whole pressure of the penal laws, we have discovered an agent almost sufficiently powerful to shake the faith of martyrs. And certainly, were it not for the steady zeal of their instructors, joined to that firm opposition of mind to which oppression ever gives additional permanency, supported also, as we confide, by the arm of Providence, the Catholics of England must long since have disappeared from the face of the earth. Penalties, discouragements, and disqualifications, with the aspersions of malevolence, and the ridicule of ignorance, make deep impressions on the stoutest minds: They will often prove an overmatch

match even for uncommon resolution and conviction.

To withstand the powerful influence of all these causes, I find little else assigned but a supposed indefatigable ardour of a few Priests. Ignorance alone can lay any stress on this puerile argument. If the Catholic Priesthood ever possessed that astonishing ascendency, which is ascribed to them, it is now at least evident, that such times are no more. Men, I believe, of every religious persuasion, have the common passions of human nature; and I am too well-acquainted with the general characters of Priests and the circumstances of things, to admit a ridiculous supposition. I shall speak more appositely to this point hereafter. In the mean-time, I must observe how replete with absurdity that idea is, which can fancy, that the learning and attention of Protestant Ministers, assisted by all the weight and interested influence of an established Church, must give way to the imposing arts, as they are called, of an inconsiderable number of Priests! Human nature, as I have observed, in all her ways most perfectly similar, here wantonly departs from order

der and the fixed line of action, to gratify, it seems, the folly of some, and the bad zeal of others.

Nothing then surely is to be feared from the number of Catholics. Let us however see, whether they may not make up by their wealth and landed interest that deficiency which, it may now be owned, must be the natural effect of numeral weakness. What Jupiter despaired of doing by other means, he compassed in a shower of gold.

THE man, who is capable of thought, and who, from thought, can form a judgment, will not be induced to believe that English Catholics can be possessed of riches. They have not, he will say, discovered the Philosopher's Stone; nor does it appear, his Catholic Majesty has yet allowed them to enter the mines of Potosi: Precluded from the Army, the Church, the Bar, and from every place of trust or profit under government, they have no means of acquiring, of improving, or of retrieving, a fortune. The Pope indeed is rich. But it is not usual with the See of Rome to bestow her earthly commodities: She receives, but does not give.

We have, at this day, but eight Peers, nineteen Baronets, and about a hundred and fifty Gentlemen of landed property.—Among the first, the Duke of Norfolk, the Earl of Shrewsbury, and the Lords Arundel and Petre, are in possession of considerable estates. But the Earl of Surrey, the eldest and only son to the Duke, having lately conformed, the large possessions of that noble and ancient family will soon fall into Protestant hands. The eldest son of Lord Teynham has also left the religion of his father.—Among the Baronets are not more than three great estates: Sir Thomas Gascoigne has this year also taken the oaths. Of the remaining Commoners, with an exception of four or five, the greatest part have not, on an average, more than one thousand pounds per annum, in landed property. Within this year alone, we have lost more by the defection of the two mentioned Gentlemen, than we have gained by Proselytes since the Revolution.

In

In trade very few fortunes have been made; and at this hour, there are not more than two Catholics of any note who are even engaged in mercantile bufinefs. The eldeft fons of our Gentry never think of trade; and the younger children have feldom a fufficient fortune, on which to ground any profpect of fuccefs. They therefore generally chufe to remain ufelefs and dependent Beings among their relations and friends, or to eat a hardly-earned and fcanty bread in the fervice of fome foreign Prince. England, like a cruel ftepmother, refufes to give them nourifhment. Should America win the great ftake, fhe now fo unjuftly contends for, good policy will doubtlefs teach her to open her ports to all religions.—Some few gain a decent livelihood by the profeffion of medicine, though, in ftrictnefs of penal juftice, they may not even be apothecaries; and others in the low walks of the law. Were they freely allowed to fell drugs, their drugs, it is well known, would be poifon; and the open practice of law would very foon transfer all Proteftant property into the hands of Catholics!

The lower classes in life, like other subjects, support themselves and families, by the common arts of industry and labour. They thank Heaven it never entered into the breast of some stern Legiflator to restrain them even from that privilege. He might have discovered, that neither the corn which was sown, nor the tree which was planted, by a Popish hand, ever arrived to maturity in Protestant soil. It is, however, certain, that were the laws against Recusants strictly executed, all the sweat of their brows would not discharge the penalties, to which the practice of their religion exposes them.

This being the state of Catholics, where are we to look for their riches. Even the estates, they are now masters of, are daily decreasing, from very obvious causes. There is a vanity of dress, equipage, and of general expence, which has seized all ranks of life. The Catholics are weak enough to give into the common folly. They live, and they spend like their neighbours, not reflecting that what they once dissipate, can by no means be retrieved. The necessary consequence is, that in a very few years, the greatest part of their

present

present possessions must fall into other hands. A Catholic, whom the love of dissipation or of fashionable life calls up to London, should be shut up by his friends in some place of secure confinement: Posterity would be deeply thankful for the kind service. Yet, as among Protestants, so are there among Catholics, Gentlemen of easy fortune who live wholly in the country, not dissipating, but doing much good with the produce of their estates; and their doors are encompassed with the blessings of their neighbours.

Still, however, there subsists an unmeaning cry; That Catholics have money always at hand to forward the growth of Popery, by opening and endowing Schools, by encouraging Proselytes, and by purchasing estates, whereby is to be acquired great parliamentary interest.—The want of religious zeal is, I believe, a strong bar to one attempt, and the want of money is a certain security against the others.

There is another instrument also, which takes away their property more effectually than the highwayman's pistol. This is the annual land-tax act, whereby each

Catholic

Catholic is loaded with the payment of a sum *double* to that affessed on Protestants. Some attempts have been made to procure relief from this heavy weight; but as yet there is not sufficient generosity in the breasts of Englishmen, to grant so small a favour, though the change could not possibly be felt by the Protestant public. Drained by this hard imposition, Catholics, in common with other subjects, are yet loaded with those taxes, which even the most wealthy Protestants now affect to say, are become intolerable.—Will malevolent and ignorant men still maintain that Catholics are rich!

Their Character.

IN point of manners and of moral character, they differ little from other men in the same walks of life. Their foreign education, it is sometimes thought, gives them at first a peculiar cast; but a free intercourse with the world soon rubs off those acute angles, unless when inveterate habits have been formed, or the mind has been peculiarly narrowed. Some years back, when the penal laws were more strictly executed, and when weak men feared some noxious contagion from the

the breath of Catholics, they associated very little with the world. A certain sternness of temper was the natural effect of this retirement; and if, in their turn, they felt a strong dislike to Protestants, it was what the conduct of the latter deserved. Some good, however, and that of no trifling consideration, was from thence derived. The estates of Catholics were in better condition; they supported with more becoming liberality their indigent and oppressed neighbours; and in the duties of religion they were greatly more sincere. The diminution of piety and of honest virtue which now prevails, is, in my opinion, but poorly compensated by the tinsel acquirements of a more polished life. Nor, after all, has one effect been obtained, which it was natural to expect. Many Protestants, though they daily converse with Catholics on the easy footing of private friendship, still retain the same general prejudices against them, which the lowest ignorance should now blush at. They can think well enough of individuals; but nothing, they tell you, can be more shocking and absurd than the principles of the body, and nothing more vicious and inimical to the duties of society

than

than their general conduct and habits of mind. It is vain to reason with such determined prejudice. Why Catholics, on their side, should entertain more liberal and just sentiments of Protestants, is a problem, I shall not solve. The fact itself is evidenced by hourly experience; and I trust, our principles as men, and our belief as Christians, are at all times as good as theirs.

The characters of the common people are hardly distinguishable from those of their neighbours. If there be any difference, the balance should rather ponderate in favour of Catholics; because, I know they are more carefully instructed in their youth, and are afterwards much attended to. They are solely to blame, if they neglect such means of moral improvement, as are constantly laid before them. It is a serious complaint in the Protestant Church, that this most important of all duties is greatly neglected. As a friend to society I must always think well of that religion, though it were crouded with many speculative absurdities, whose Ministers are attentive to the instruction of youth.

The

The lives of Catholics, in general, are observed to be regular: and without panegyrizing their virtues, to which I am not inclined, I only beg Protestants themselves to declare their sentiments. Do they know, in the whole extent of his Majesty's dominions, better men, better citizens, or better subjects; people more amenable to the laws, or more observant of all the duties of civil life? Their charities, as far as their powers of doing good extend, are great. Every object in distress is a fellow-creature who calls for relief; nor do I know, that Catholics ever make any distinction of persons, unless (which has sometimes happened) when Protestants have first refused assistance to those of the Popish persuasion.

From Gentry thus dissipated, as the most extravagant Protestants, or else temperate and retired, as the most moderate, and from a commonalty peaceable, virtuous, and honest, what has the most guarded and suspicious government to apprehend?

Their Abilities.

NOR are the natural acquired abilities of Catholics at all calculated to intimidate, from any suspicion that, should an occasion offer, they might either form, or attempt to execute, some grand design for the subversion of this Protestant government. In this regard, they are rather, I think, below, than above, the common level. As their education is inferior to that of Protestants, and as afterwards in life, they have few inducements to improve their understandings by such application, as can alone give superiority to mental talents, they generally rest satisfied with that small pittance of knowledge, which some foreign College originally supplied. Where circumstances allow it, they have perhaps travelled—and so have their portmanteaus. Under the tutelage of some ignorant, and consequently self-sufficient Priest, the youth has seen objects of vast curiosity; he has kissed the Pope's slipper, and he has visited our Lady at Loretto. Thus qualified he returns, and it is well, if he brings not with him many of the follies, and some of the vices, of the countries he has passed through.—However, abstracting from the *pious* part of improvement, which they do not pretend

tend to, Proteſtant Gentlemen have little more to ſhew from their travels, than the ſons of Catholics.

Though the want of education, I complain of, or rather a total inattention to improvement afterwards, be an inſurmountable bar to the acquiſition of great accompliſhments, yet ſo very deficient is the preſent generation of Catholics, that few of them ſeem to poſſeſs thoſe native talents, which often fall to the lot of unimproved mortality. From them the Proteſtant conſtitution of England is, I am ſure, in no danger. But for the honour, and for the utility, of the Catholic Body, we have much reaſon to repine at this untoward circumſtance. The petitions of a ſuffering people are often not attended to by thoſe who can give relief, becauſe they are not preſented, or purſued, with that ſpirit of manly firmneſs and commanding eloquence, which will find their way even to the throne. We are a diſunited body, and ever have been ſo. They who ſhould take the lead, are either unable or unwilling to act; and the body ſuffers by the indolence, the little views, or the timidity of their leaders. It has been seen in the preceding pages, how often the best-concerted schemes have been totally frustrated by some foolish or wayward opposition.——I mean not the severity of these reflections should be applied universally to all: We have, amongst us, men of real merit and of strong endowments; but it is generally the fate, as it is the wish, of these, to be kept back from the eye of public observation.

We have reason, indeed, to lament the loss of a young Nobleman, who very lately, as I mentioned, is gone over to the Protestant side. From nature he had received talents, adequate to the greatest designs, and to these talents he had given some cultivation. But there is in him a cast, a singularity of mind, and a *bizarrerie* of thought, which must ever give a tinge to the fairest endowments. With abilities equal to the management of great public business, his best ambition will spend itself in vain declamation against men and measures. He was always fond of opposition. I knew him when a boy; and at that time, to thwart, if possible, by petty controversy, the views of his masters, to complain of undue influence, to

magnify

magnify grievances, and to head a little band of malecontents, were the objects truly congenial with his humour. With a less restless, less inconsistent, and less dissipated mind (for dissipation has now greatly added to his native character) he would have mounted with ardour to the first place, at the head of a body of men, to which his birth and his abilities called him. Here was a field wide enough for the display of the greatest talents. He might have given splendor to the Catholic cause; would have possessed their warmest affections; and might have asked relief for himself and for them in a style, that would have commanded attention. If his soul was not large enough to grasp at this high pre-eminence, and if, from insensibility to the impressions of religion, his conscience is sincere, I blame him not, that he has deserted the cause of his Ancestors; but I pity an Earl of S———y, who can sink down to the paltry service of a party-declaimer in the Lower House of parliament.

It is a singular circumstance in the Ecclesiastical history of this country, that in proportion as a man loses all sense of religion,

ligion, and becomes immoral, he sees before him a better prospect of enjoying all the privileges of the established Church. I never knew an instance, in which conviction of the errors of Popery has made one Proselyte. They become Protestants, as soon as they cease almost to be Christians. It must surely be a bad arrangement, which thus exposes to oppression the sincere and the virtuous, and which opens to the vicious and dissipated man the road of ease, of honour, and of preferment.

It may be expected, whilst the pencil is still in my hand, that I should give a sketch at least of some principal characters, which remain amongst us. It must not be supposed, that the noble Lord, I have mentioned, has carried off with him all the mental worth of the party. When Æneas tore one golden branch from the mystic tree, it was instantly supplied by another,

  Primo avulso non deficit alter
Aureus; & simili frondescit virga metallo.
         Virg.

But I am not expert in the art of colouring, and plain delineation might perhaps

haps offend. The most faithful portraits are not always the most pleasing. The public, which well knows how to appreciate merit, is in possession of the originals. If nature has been too thrifty in her gifts, or if circumstances have rather contributed to lull, than to rouse, the faculties of their minds, their condition should not be censured. The most brilliant talents often prove less serviceable than those of a more fixed texture. Even in the works of art, lead and iron are sometimes preferred to more splendid metals. Lead indeed loses with difficulty its well-known character; but iron may be hardened into steel.—*Fangar vice cotis.* I wish I could stimulate some of my acquaintance to a more active exertion of those powers, which they have; and which disuse in a short time may perhaps torpify for ever.

IT has been seen with what firm attachment, Catholics adhered to the house of Stuarts. There was something in that loyalty, which even bordered on infatuation. They had received no favours from them; and experience said, they were not to expect any. Conviction of its rectitude

Their Political Sentiments.

titude was therefore the only motive which gave stability to their affection. At the accession of his present Majesty, some few Catholics were still intoxicated with the fumes of Jacobitism; nor did it then seem they could be easily expelled. By one of those singular revolutions, however, for which no cause can be assigned, in the small space of a few years, the distemper worked off; and when the oath of allegiance was tendered in 1778, hardly, I believe, one Catholic refused to take it. It was a capricious event, but to such human nature is often subject.—It may not be inferred, that a change so sudden should not be relied on: For, I am clearly sensible, that Catholics are now as sincere in their attachment to the Hanover family, as they ever were to the Stuarts. Of this they would give the most convincing proofs, were they permitted to attest their allegiance by the common exertions of other subjects.—After all, I see no very particular grounds for this new disposition. We have yet received but little relief; and we continue an oppressed and injured people. The boasted excellencies of the British constitution are nothing to me, who am deprived of the common right rights of humanity; they only serve to make my condition more irksome, and to create a restless desire of changes and revolutions. My situation cannot be worse, and it may be mended.

In the present state of contending parties, it is curious to see how Catholics shape their politics. It is the cry of *Opposition*, that they are friends to court measures; that they aim to join their interest to that of the crown; and that against the rights of the people they will ever be ready to strengthen the arm of Prerogative. As this evidently is the language of party, it merits little notice. Catholics are as free to form opinions as other men; and in their general decisions I see the same rule of conduct invariably followed. In their politics is the same discordance and variation of sentiment, as is elsewhere observable. Ignorance only can assert the contrary belief. If, on the whole, they be rather inclined to government, which I think is the case, they have good reasons for their choice. It would be extreme folly to set their faces against that power, from which ultimately all redress must be derived. Besides, they feel not those incentives to opposition, which are known to actuate the breasts of many Protestants.——It is false, that they are friends to arbitrary power. They smart too severely under the rod of oppression, to wish to give it additional strength in the hands of a tyrant. Why even, as is often asserted, should they, from any previous principle, be more inclined to monarchy, than to any other form of government? At this day, there are Catholic republics, and Catholic states of every description. In the annals of this nation, never were there stouter champions for liberty, than the ancient Barons. *Magna Charta* is of Catholic growth. Nor do I know, that the boasting Protestant Patriots, of the present hour, would have acted at *Runimede* with more manly firmness, though their lips, I doubt not, might have distilled more copious streams of honeyed eloquence.——Catholics are instructed to submit themselves to the ruling powers, and not wantonly to engage in faction. The murmurs of disappointed or of disaffected men can seldom be reconciled with reason and the plain dictates of religion.—We acknowledge ourselves much indebted to some Gentlemen in *Opposition*, and

and we hope to experience the continuance of their favourable exertions; but in us it would be a conduct highly censurable, were we to adopt the language of party, with a view of making an adulatory tender of services, in themselves too weak and insufficient to effect any real purpose.

It is but lately that Catholics have at all appeared to engage in politics: they were too depressed for the exertions of men; and even now they scarcely take any decided part. In my opinion, such torpid indifference is reprehensible. I would not be factious, but I would shew that I had some property at stake, and that I wished to see it well defended. We have hitherto gained little by a long course of inactive submission. An Englishman should at all times dare to speak his sentiments. These at least cannot be shackled, and a *Trimmer* between two parties generally meets the contempt of both.

If Catholics be capable of doing any injury to the state, which, as it is, they are; surely they are also capable of serving it, in the same proportion. It is unjust, therefore, if Magistrates, by a tend—

hient measures, to insure their affections. Should they be incapable of resenting ill usage (and experience has sufficiently declared such to be their lowly condition) how unmanly is it, to oppress the weak and defenceless! They are to a man loyal, sincere, and patriotic; they have given the most solemn security for their allegiance, in this they have done all that men can do; and having done this, they are intitled to the privileges of subjects, and to the protection of the laws.

Their Religion.

IT is therefore in religious matters only that Catholics hold opinions different from those of Protestant Englishmen. Here they pretend not to think as they do; and this candid declaration should give evidence in favour of their general professions. The insincere man would affect coincidence in opinion, as well in religion as in politics, at least when his interest required it; and it will hardly be said, that we should not be benefited by an artful disguise of our religious belief. We declare then our dissent from many parts of the Protestant creed; and we openly avow our faith in

articles

articles, which the reformed Church has utterly exploded.

Liberty of thought is essential to human nature. Take that away, and man, his organization alone excepted, will not be superior to the ass which browses on the thistle, or to the thistle which vegetates from the earth: It is that only which he can strictly call his own, because no created power can deprive him of it. His property may be taken away by the hand of violence, and his person may be thrown into confinement; but in the dungeons of the Bastile his thoughts are still free, and out of the reach of tyranny.—There is no subject on which our thoughts may not range, and on which they may not judge. For what other end, was such extent given to the mental powers? When we abuse these faculties, by an improper display, we become responsible to the Being who gave them to us; but to him only.—In religious enquiries why is our reason to be particularly restrained? As the subject is of singular importance, it seems, even greater latitude should be allowed us. Is it your business to invade the best privilege I enjoy?—With this conviction of mind I examine, I judge, and I chuse my own religion. It is the affair of my own conscience; it is a concern betwixt myself and God; and it belongs to no other to arraign my conduct, or to censure my determination. To molest me then in the practice of such duties, as my conscience again tells me I should perform, is an equal stretch of tyranny.

On these principles, to me of clearest evidence, is founded the Christian doctrine of *Toleration*; a doctrine, which only ignorance of the rights of mankind, ecclesiastical domination, or blind enthusiasm, could ever controvert. If I dissent from other men; do not they also dissent from me? And if I chuse to submit my faith to the decisions of the Catholic Church, I use no other liberty than he does, who chuses to reject them.—Catholics, I know, have often denied the external practice of religion to sectaries; they now continue to do so in many countries. It is not my intention to justify what is ill-done. But, to be intolerant is a leading maxim of every established Church; whether it have its seat in England or in France, in Hindostan or in China. It is now time to correct

correct abuses, and not to seek excuse for our own, from the example of others. All are equally censurable; and when English Protestants arraign so severely the intolerance of Rome, they only mark out more pointedly the injustice of their own conduct.

At all events, what has state-policy to do with the concern of a man's conscience? If he obey the laws of his country, and perform the duties of a subject, the demands of the civil magistrate are complied with. Is he to say, "You shall not wear a sword for the defence of your person or property, because you chuse to pray for the repose of the soul of your deceased father; or, if you will not think as I do, I forbid you to approach within ten miles of the capital?"—This surely is a species of sottish tyranny, which could only be exercised at a time, when to be absurd in the extreme was the first endowment of a statesman.

When it is found that any sect of men profess principles in religion, which either tend to the destruction of social happiness, or are incompatible with the established order

order of government, it will not be denied, that the most rigorous means should be used for their suppression. The sword of justice should be drawn, and the miscreants be exterminated. It was thus, the Saxon Edgar freed this kingdom from the ravages of wolves, by which it was once infested. Yet Lithe to, I believe, no men have ever professed such destructive tenets. The religion of every man teaches him to be good, and he would be so, were he to comply with its injunctions. The enemies to a sect may charge them falsly, and their misrepresentations may impose on the ignorant. Instructions should be taken from the well-informed, and not from the cry of defamation. I will apply to a man's own heart for an account of his tenets.—No people have suffered so much from slanderous description, as Catholics. They have repeatedly laid their belief before the public; which, with great humanity, always refuses to give credit to their declarations. You shall believe us, they say—but we will not believe you. I suspect there must be some secret motive for this incredulity. For it is the disposition of a virtuous mind not to doubt the assertions of honest men. The liar thinks no man can speak truth—becauſe he never does it himſelf.

Once more I will give my reader a conciſe, but accurate expoſition of Catholic belief. It is contained in few propoſitions. Should it vary from any previous opinions of his own; I only beg he will think, that I know better than he does, what is my own religion. The requeſt is modeſt.— The following rule I muſt inſiſt he will attend to, becauſe it is the grand criterion, by which each article of our faith may be diſtinctly aſcertained.

THIS rule is—*All that and only that belongs to Catholic belief, which is revealed in the word of God, and which is propoſed by the Catholic Church to all its members, to be believed with divine faith.* Rule of Faith and Articles.

Guided by this certain *criterion* we profeſs to believe,

1. That Chriſt has eſtabliſhed a Church upon earth, and that this Church is that, which holds communion with the See of Rome, being One, Holy, Catholic, and Apoſtolical.

2. That

2. That we are obliged to hear this Church; and therefore that she is infallible, by the guidance of Almighty God, in her decisions regarding faith.

3. That Saint Peter, by divine commission, was appointed the head of this Church, under Christ its founder: And that the Pope, or Bishop of Rome, as successor to Saint Peter, has always been, and is at present, by divine right, head of this Church.

4. That the Canon of the Old and New Testament, as proposed to us by this Church, is the word of God; as also such traditions, belonging to faith and morals, which being originally delivered by Christ to his Apostles, have been preserved, by constant succession, in the Catholic Church.

5. That honour and veneration are due to the Angels of God and his Saints; that they offer up prayers to God for us; that it is good and profitable to have recourse to their intercession; and that the relics or earthly remains of God's particular servants are to be held in respect.

6. That

6. That no sins ever were, or can be, remitted, unless by the mercy of God, thro' Jesus Christ; and therefore that man's justification is the work of divine grace.

7. That the good works, which we do, receive their whole value from the grace of God; and that by such works, we not only comply with the precepts of the divine law, but that we thereby likewise merit eternal life.

8. That by works, done in the spirit of Penance, we can make satisfaction to God, for the temporal punishment, which often remains due, after our sins, by the divine goodness, have been forgiven us.

9. That Christ has left to his Church a power of granting indulgences, that is, a relaxation from such temporal chastisement only as remains due after the divine pardon of sin; and that the use of such indulgences is profitable to sinners.

10. That there is a Purgatory or middle State; and that the souls of imperfect Christians therein detained are helped by the prayers of the faithful.

11. That

11. That there are seven Sacraments, all instituted by Christ; Baptism, Confirmation, Eucharist, Penance, Extreme Unction, Holy Order, Matrimony.

12. That in the most holy Sacrament of the Eucharist, there is truly, really, and substantially, the body and blood, together with the soul and the divinity of our Lord Jesus Christ.

13. That in this sacrament there is, by the omnipotence of God, a conversion, or change, of the whole substance of the bread into the body of Christ, and of the whole substance of the wine into his blood; which change we call Transubstantiation.

14. That under either kind Christ is received whole and entire.

15. That in the Mass, or Sacrifice of the Altar, is offered to God a true, proper, and propitiatory sacrifice for the living and the dead.

16. That in the Sacrament of Penance, the sins we fall into after baptism are, by the divine mercy, forgiven us.

These

These are the great points of Catholic belief, by which we are distinguished from other Christian Societies; and these only are the real and essential tenets of our Religion. We admit also the other grand articles of revealed and natural religion, which the gospel and the light of reason have manifested to us. To these we submit as Men and as Christians, and to the former as obedient children of the Catholic Church.

Reader, have you weighed attentively the plain and obvious meaning of these articles? And do you think there is one, which merits to be treated with such harsh censure, as is generally given them? Do you think there is one, the belief of which should, in a Christian country, restrain us from the common privileges of subjects and the blessings of unbounded Toleration? I mean not to say, that our doctrine is of such evidence as to command conviction and instant belief. This is a very different question; nor do I speak of the *truth* of our religion: Were it *false* in every article, my reasoning would be the same.—Tenets which to Catholics, from the long acquired habits of education, may seem familiar and highly rational, are not therefore calculated to make the same impression on those, to whom they are new and uninteresting. The friend to truth will maturely weigh the important object, and will decide, as reason and the bias of genuine Christianity shall appear to preponderate. Of this, however, I am convinced that, were certain obstacles removed, such as the views of interest, the animosity of party, the blindness of prejudice, and those thick clouds which controversy has raised, it would then appear, that the Protestant Church of England and Catholics are divided by very thin partitions.

There are points of discipline also, which regulate conduct, and to which we pay obedience; as fasting on particular days, communion in one kind, celibacy of churchmen, use of the Latin language in public service, and other similar practices; but as these vary, and may be either altered or suppressed by due authority, they belong not to what is properly styled the *Faith* of Catholics.

Opinions also, whether regarding belief or practice, of particular schools or of particular

ticular divines, constitute a distinct and separate object. Great latitude in the forming of such opinions is allowed; and consequently it will be often abused. It has been in the power of some men to give an undue weight to such opinions, whereby Catholics themselves have been too often imposed on. They have ignorantly confounded the inventions of fallible men with the unerring declarations of Heaven. Of this circumstance our enemies have many times taken an unfair advantage, and the faith of Catholics has suffered from the false representation.— Some opinions may deserve respect, but others should be despised and reprobated. And it should be noticed, that most of the charges brought against us are founded on this false supposition, *that the opinions of private men, or particular divines, are as much a part of our religion, as the articles I have stated.* When all this extraneous matter, whether of discipline or of opinion is brought to a proper test, by the rules I have laid down such insist on, it will soon appear in what light it is to be considered. Were I to reject every opinion, hitherto discovered, and solely adhere to the articles of doctrine as I have stated, I should be a *Catholic* in the strict and accurate acceptation of the word. Divines might censure me, Casuists might defame me, and the Pope might deny me the name of *Papist*; but my faith would still be pure, unimpaired, and Catholic.

Charges against them

NOTWITHSTANDING this clear description of Catholic belief, many charges, of a very black and defamatory complexion, are perpetually urged against them; nor has it been possible to silence the voice of calumny.

It has been very recently asserted, that though we have taken an oath of allegiance and fidelity, we should not be tolerated in a Protestant country, because we have yet given no *security* for our good behaviour. It is a fixed maxim, say these men of refined discernment, in the Church of Rome, to which they all universally subscribe, " That no faith is to be kept with heretics; That the Pope can dispense with all oaths; and that every Priest has a discretionary power to forgive sins of every description."

We

We have answered; That we reject such doctrine as impious and unchristian; that it was never admitted by Catholics; that if any private person believed it, he was a bad man; and that no power, of whatever denomination, could make it lawful to violate such engagements, though contracted with Heretics, Jews, Turks, or Infidels.

We have answered; That we do not hold, the Pope has power to dispense with oaths; that the exercise of such power would be a violation of the unalterable laws of justice and truth; that it would be impious and invalid; and that no decisions, even of General Councils, can annul the sacred obligation of such engagements.

We have answered; That Priests have not a discretionary power to forgive sins; that to the sinner, who comes to them with *all* the dispositions of sincere repentance, we do believe they can, by the appointment of Heaven, grant absolution; but that it is *God alone*, who *interiorly* absolves the penitent, whilst his Ministers *exteriorly* exercise the function.

When

When we are accused of teaching that the Pope can depose Kings, and free their subjects from their allegiance; our answer is; That we abhor such maxims; that if Popes have sometimes exercised a deposing power, we condemn their conduct; that, as we acknowledge in him powers of spiritual jurisdiction only, we admit no interference from his court in the temporal concerns of state; and that we would oppose any secular attempts from him, with the same alacrity, as we would those of a French invader.

It is still urged, that we allow in him an extent of jurisdiction, which is not consistent with the established government of this realm.

With regard to that particular arrangement, which appoints the King head of the Church, we avow, it is true, our dissent from it. But as that relates only to the established Church, of which we are not members, our conduct is the same as that of other Dissenters, over whom his Majesty claims no ecclesiastical jurisdiction.—The Bishop of Rome is our principal superior, as he is the supreme head of the Catholic Church. But all his power, being wholly *spiritual*, has no relation to civil government; it reaches to such matters as, we think, appertain not to the controul of Princes.—The state of religion with us is so very low and imperfect, that it is not easy to discover, wherein the Pope has room for the exercise of any part of his prerogative. We have no national Church, and we guide ourselves by the rule of ancient practice and discipline.——In Catholic countries must be looked for the proper display of the Papal power; and it will be found that its sphere of action is extremely bounded. They acknowledge in him a *primacy* of jurisdiction; but it is a primacy subjected to the controul of Canons and to the general order of established laws. His power is in no sense absolute. It is his duty to attend to the execution of established laws, and to take care that the Christian republic receive no injury. This is the office of a first magistrate in every well-regulated state. And to shew how limited his authority really is; we maintain that each Pastor in his parish, each Bishop in his diocese, each Metropolitan in his province, and each Patriarch in his nation,

nation, is possessed of a proper and essential jurisdiction, wholly uncontroulable by, and independent of, the See of Rome. They respect his primacy, but they have their rights and liberties as ancient and as sacred as are his own. Such was the order divinely established by Christ. The canonical *instalment* of Bishops and other higher Ministers is alone a branch of the Papal jurisdiction.——I know that, in former times principally, the Popes have exerted a very undue stretch of power. They had the passions of men; and the Christian world was too weak and too ignorant to oppose them. The consequences were at last fatal. It is vain to suppose that any establishments, committed to human direction, can be long free from abuses: It is our duty, by prudent and the most effectual means, to contribute to their reformation.—Such, as I have described, is the nature of the jurisdiction of Rome, and being such, England, I am very confident, has no reason to fear we shall ever aim to introduce a power incompatible with her privileges.

When we have been called Idolaters; we knew not what was meant by the charge:

charge: For to God alone we pay our homage of *adoration*; but we think that particular *respect* is due to the first and best of his creatures.

We are accused of great uncharitableness in allowing Salvation to none but Catholics.—But this also is a mistaken notion. We say, I believe, no more, than do all other Christian Societies. Religion certainly is an affair of very serious consideration. When therefore a man, either neglects to inform himself, or when informed, refuses to follow the conviction of his mind, such a one, we say, is not in the way of Salvation. After mature enquiries, if I am convinced that the religion of England is the only true one, am I not obliged to become a Protestant? In similar circumstances, must not you likewise declare yourself a Catholic? Our meaning is, that no one can be saved out of the true Church; and as we consider the evidence of the truth of our religion to be great, that he who will not embrace truth, when he sees it, deserves not to be happy. God however is the searcher of hearts; he only can read those internal dispositions,

dispositions, on which rectitude of conduct alone depends.

Such are the answers, we have always given to these, and to other similar charges. We know, we have had amongst us many bad and weak men, who have often spoken and often acted wrong; but it is unfair to involve the innocent in the ways of the guilty. By this *ordeal*, the virtues and good qualities of every society upon earth would be utterly done away.—As Christians, therefore, we admit all the doctrines of divine Revelation; as Catholics, we submit our faith to the authority of that Church, which we think Christ has founded; as men, we profess our obedience to the moral precepts of reason and nature; and as subjects, the King has our allegiance, the laws our reverence, and the state may command our services.

Their Priests.

THE account I have given of the religion of Catholics naturally leads me to their Ministers. On this head I could wish to supply all possible information. Popish Priests are generally considered as a fair game, at which the shafts of satire and

and malevolence may be thrown with impunity. Like other objects, this also has two sides: The equitable spectator will wish to view both.

By an arrangement, which took place in the reign of James the Second, England was divided into four districts, and a Bishop was appointed to preside over each. They had then 1000l. per ann. settled on each of them, out of the Exchequer: but this only continued till the Revolution, when they were reduced to the necessity of supporting themselves by the best means in their power. Since that time, the same regulation with regard to numbers has continued; and as they have no particular place of residence allotted, each Bishop generally chuses to live in the most centrical and convenient situation. Their office is, to attend to the small concerns of their respective districts; to administer the Sacrament of Confirmation; to provide the different congregations with Priests; and to take care that these perform their duties, and behave in a manner becoming the character of Churchmen. It has been said by a peevish writer, " That *Popish Bishops* go about, and exercise every

part

part of their function, without offence, and without observation." This is an unfair representation: For it is in the most private manner that any part of their function is exercised; and as they possess none of the insignia of the Episcopal order, their *goings about* do not distinguish them from other men. Could modern Christians be inspired with the holy ambition of emulating the virtues of the apostolic ages, our Catholic Bishops have, surely, the noblest field before them. They are not exposed to the allurements of worldly temptations; and all their treasures are in heaven. One hundred pounds per annum is more than equal to the revenue of their Episcopal Sees. Will the author of the *Confessional*, from whom the above remark is taken, be willing to exchange his *Archdeaconry* of Cleveland for the *Mitre* of these Popish Bishops?

As far as I can rely on my information, which I think is accurate, the number of Priests, now employed, is about 360. Their distribution is as follows.—In the northern district, which takes in the counties of Northumberland, Cumberland, Westmoreland, Durham, York, Lancaster, and

and Chester, there are about 167. Of these 48 are Ex-Jesuits. Three places are now vacant. This district contains the greatest number of Priests, and also the greatest number of Catholics; but not in proportion to the number of Clergy; many being private Chaplains to Gentlemen, where there are no congregations. Since their dissolution, nine places have been given up by the Ex-Jesuits, two of which are not likely ever to be revived.

In the midland district, are about 90 Priests; 28 of whom are Ex-Jesuits. There are now fourteen places vacant. This district declines very fast, as appears from the great number of congregations now without Priests. Most of these have been vacant for some time, and no Clergymen unengaged have hitherto been found to supply them; though some of them are Gentlemen's houses; by which means some families are obliged to go from five to ten miles, on Sundays, to Chapel. It may be noticed that this district, though composed of the greatest number of counties, and those mostly large, to the amount of sixteen, contains only 8,460 Catholics, which is computed to be about two thirds of what there were thirty or forty years ago.

The western district contains about 44 Priests; 23 are Ex-Jesuits. There is one place vacant, and has been so for some time; no person can be found to occupy it. This district is the thinnest of Catholics of any in England, though its extent be great. It contains eight English counties, and the whole of North and South-Wales.

The London district, comprising nine counties, has 58 Priests; 11 are Ex-Jesuits. There are five places vacant. This district has also diminished, and is declining very fast.

These Priests, whose number and distribution I have given, either live as Chaplains in the families of Gentlemen, and have the care of the little congregations round them; or else they reside in towns, or in some country-places, where funds have been settled for their support. The Chapels are in their own houses. From many places being now vacant, as I have noticed, where Priests were formerly kept, it is evident that their number is greatly on the decrease. The Jesuits also are daily dying away; nor is there any succession to supply their places. In the lapse of a few years, we shall see a very great additional falling off. Never, surely, was there a wilder fancy than the common cry of the growth of Popery, and of the great influx of Priests, since the passing of the late act in favour of Catholics!

Voluntary poverty is generally esteemed a virtue of high evangelical merit; but when involuntary, it loses its meritorious character, and may be ranked among the miseries of human life. If Catholic Priests are disposed to make a virtue of necessity, like their Bishops, they will meet with no obstacle in their progress to perfection. Twenty pounds per annum is thought a very handsome salary for a Gentleman's Chaplain; and if the rural curate have twenty more, to keep himself, his horse, and his servant, it will be said, he is very well provided. Some may have small annuities from their own families; but this is not common.—From men thus broken by penury, the frowns of an imperious patron, or by hard labour in the service of their neighbour, government has little reason, I think.

think, to apprehend machinations against the state; nor should the established Church envy their condition, or tremble for the subversion of her Hierarchy.

Our Priests, in their general character, are upright and sincere: But narrowed by a bad education, they contract early prejudices, which they very seldom afterwards deposite. The theological lumber of the schools supplies, in their minds, the place of more useful furniture. Moderately skilled in the Latin and Greek languages, they know nothing of their own; nor do they become sensible of their manifold deficiencies, till it be too late to attempt improvement. They are bred up in the persuasion that, on coming to England, they are to meet with racks and persecution: They land, therefore, as in an enemy's country, cautious, diffident, and suspectful. A man truly orthodox flies heretical company; he fears to be contaminated; and he would not receive instruction from so foul a source. A Priest is seldom seen in the society of Protestants. The Catholics, he is told to herd with, either are unable to improve him, or if able, they are seldom willing. Contracted

in

in his circumstances, he has not the means of drawing information from books; and unfashioned in the forms of elegant life, his company is not asked for. Thus denied all occasions of improvement, if his native dispositions will allow him, he soon sits down sullenly contented, and looks no further. If he ever had abilities, disuse will, in a short time, lay them asleep; and at sixty he will be found the same man he was at twenty-five.—It is the complaint of our Gentry, that Priests are rough and unsociable: They would be less so, perhaps, if their patrons were less proud, less ignorant, and less imperious. On both sides are faults, which should be corrected. That day is passed, when the counsel of the Priesthood was officiously sought after; when, from the cottage to the throne, it pervaded every department in life. The employment did not make them better men; and their employers are deservedly styled ignorant and weak-minded bigots. A Churchman who, in the discharge of his duty, is regular, exemplary, and manly, must be respected; if he be ill-treated, it will only be by such, whose frowns will do him more honour than their smiles.

It is often said, that Popish Priests have an unbounded zeal for making Proselytes. Were it true, I see no reproach in the charge. It proves that they are sincere in their religious belief; that they esteem themselves in the best way; and that they wish to impart to others the important truths of salvation. The man of zeal, and only this man, will, in every religion, strive to make converts; and when evidently he is not actuated by motives of interest or some worldly pursuit, his only aim can be the good of his neighbour. If Priests ever possessed the spirit complained of, it has, I am sure, either long since evaporated, or is become very unsuccessful; for the number of those, who conform to the established Church, is far beyond those who come over to us. Real zeal is not a lasting impulse, when there is not some passion to give it strength; and in what are we benefited by an increase of numbers? To instruct those who are born Catholics; to make them good Christians and good Citizens, is a task by itself sufficiently interesting; we are already too many to suffer; and in us too many are already lost to the service of our country.

It is a very fortunate circumstance, in the discipline of the Catholic Church, that Priests are forbidden to marry. They who now can hardly maintain themselves, would not easily provide for a wife and children. Protestants often inveigh against this celibacy of our Churchmen; but it would be well, I believe, if many of theirs continued single: Where shall the unprovided offspring of a deceased Clergyman find relief from penury and distress? Luther indeed did well to condemn a practice, he was not willing to follow; and his marriage with a Nun was to his disciples a convincing proof, that celibacy was no virtue.

The influence, which Priests have it in their power still to acquire from the use of *confession*, it must be allowed, is very great. Take but once fast hold of a man's conscience, and you may lead him where you please. It is therefore, in our Church, a concern of the greatest moment, that Priests be well-instructed, and that they be good men. When this is the case, they become a powerful engine, whereby religion may be greatly advanced, and much public utility derived to the state.

Confession

Confession is a great check to vice, and it promotes the practice of virtue. It may be abused, as the best things too often are. Abstracting from all divine institution, were I to found a commonwealth, a law, obliging all my subjects to frequent confession of their sins, should be a principal ordinance. But the choice of my Priests should have my peculiar care. I would not, however, myself be found often in their company; for the Priest who holds in his hand the conscience of his Prince, too often meddles in the temporal concerns of state, which belong not to him.

The Jesuits, from the day of their institution, raised, through the Christian world, a suspicious jealousy, which they were never careful to suppress; they also raised an admiration of their zeal and of their unbounded activity. In our penal statutes they are marked out as a body of men wholly distinct from other Priests. It was thought, that they held principles inimical to the rights of mankind, and that their designs against Princes and their States were of the most deleterious complexion. There was no truth in this imagination. They had amongst them, indeed,

deed, Divines of wild fancy; they had loose and indulgent Casuists; and they had men of dangerous activity. Where the weaknesses and common passions to which our nature is subject, are allowed to operate, things could not be otherwise; and the Jesuits were not more reprehensible, than are all other societies of men. The influence, which their zeal, their soft insinuation, and their abilities, acquired them, was, in every walk of life, amazingly extensive. It was often productive of great good, and it was sometimes productive of great evil. They aspired, I think, too high; and the rapidity of their fall could only be equalled by that of their ascent. To the Protestant Church they were always particularly odious: They were purposely raised to oppose the progress, and to combat the opinions, of the first Reformers. Their attachment to the See of Rome was great; and in them the Papal prerogative had always experienced the firmest support. It was, therefore, matter of astonishment when the Roman Pontiff pronounced their dissolution. He was either a bad politician, or he was compelled to do it.—In abilities the Jesuits were thought to surpass all other

other religious orders; but because they wanted prudence to rein their ambition, and to moderate their career of power, they fell,——and were not pitied.—The English Jesuits were, I think, rather inferior to their brethren in other parts of Europe. Of this many reasons might be assigned. But there was a certain sameness in manners, and a peculiar cast of features, which generally marked every member of the Society. Among the Tea-shrubs in China, in the missions of Chili, in the gardens of Versailles, or in a cottage in Lancashire, a Jesuit was a distinguishable man.—The few still remaining, daily dying off, in the course of some years, their generation will be extinct, and their name almost forgotten. We shall then perhaps see reason to lament their suppression. At all events, it is now time to drop those idle fears, which the phantom of Jesuitical craft and machinations formerly gave rise to.

Their Schools in England.

IT was a groundless rumour, which lately prevailed, that Catholics were opening schools in all parts of the kingdom, whereby the rising generation of Protestants

ſtants were all to be perverted to the errors of Popery. The real fact is, that we have not opened one new ſchool ſince the year 1778. The whole number of thoſe which we have, are, I think, but three, at leaſt thoſe of any note. There is one in Hertfordſhire; one near Birmingham in Warwickſhire; and a third near Wolverhampton in Staffordſhire. In London are ſome day-ſchools; and in other parts may be, perhaps, little eſtabliſhments, where an old woman gives lectures on the Hornbook and the Art of Spelling. As her leſſons convey no documents of treaſon or ſedition, government need not watch her with any anxious attention.—At the two firſt mentioned ſchools are generally about twenty or thirty boys, who leave them about the age of twelve or fourteen. That in Staffordſhire is far the moſt numerous. Its deſign is to give ſome education to children of a lower claſs. They learn their religion, and ſuch other things, as may qualify them for trade and the uſual buſineſs of life. When it can be avoided, they never admit Proteſtants, from an apprehenſion that it might give offence; as alſo from a well-grounded ſuſpicion, that it would tend gradually to weaken the

Y religious

religious principles of the Catholic boys. It is to me astonishing, that Protestants can be found, who, were it in their power, would deprive us even of this small privilege of educating our own children! The ideas of such a man are a disgrace to human nature. *Ultimus suorum moriatur!* It was the wish of the ancients to their greatest enemies.

Their Foreign Schools.

SOON after the accession of Queen Elizabeth, when Catholics had lost all hopes of re-establishment; and when by severe statutes the practice of their religion was prohibited, and themselves were not allowed to receive education at home; many of them retired abroad, and, by degrees, associated into regular communities. In 1568, Dr. Allan, afterwards made Cardinal, founded a College for the English at Douay, a town in Flanders, then subject to the Spanish King; and in process of time, other Colleges and places of education were established in France, Spain, and Portugal.—The remains likewise of the religious orders, who had been dispersed at the suppression of Monasteries, collected themselves, and formed into communities.

The first object of these different establishments was, to provide Ministers for the support of their religion in England, and in a secondary view, to give education to the Catholic youth. Young men, therefore, soon repaired thither; some of them took orders, and then returned to their own country. To frustrate this scheme, which was the only means now left of preserving from utter ruin the small remains of Catholicity in England, many very severe statutes were made by Elizabeth and her successors. However, in spite of this opposition, and of the various attempts then made to prevail on the different Princes to expel them their territories, they stood, and exist to the present hour. It was surely a stretch of cruel despotism, thus to subject those, who should send their children abroad, to hard penalties, and, at the same time, not to allow them to be educated at home, unless they took oaths, which in their consciences they thought unlawful!

The men whom, for many succeeding years, these Seminaries sent into England, were very able and informed. A general spirit of enquiry, especially in matters of religion,

religion, had begun to call into life those mental powers, which, for whole centuries back, had slept in lazy indolence. Controversy became the fashionable occupation of the learned; and true religion has many obligations to their laborious efforts. The English Priests eagerly engaged in those disputes of religion with their Protestant antagonists; and from the writings they left behind them, it appears, they were well-skilled in the arts of controversy. There is indeed an acrimony and a harshness of reflection in their works, which, to judge from modern habits, would rather irritate, than produce sentiments of moderation and mutual forbearance. But this was the stern character of the age; and it may, I believe, at all times be doubted, whether the object of polemic writers is not rather to foil their adversary and to triumph, than, from the love of truth, to combat error, and to convince, from the godlike motive of doing good.

The present state of these establishments is as follows:—The College at Douay founded, as I said, in 1568, is the most considerable, and is governed by a President fident and other Superiors, all of the English nation. It belongs to the secular Clergy; and the number of students is generally above a hundred. As its design is to form Churchmen, and to give an academical education to the sons of Gentlemen, its course of studies has been consequently adapted to this double purpose. But the complaint is, that its plan is not proportioned to the present improved state of things; that the Priests, who come from thence, are ill-provided with that learning, which other Universities can now supply; and that young men, after eight years application, return home, very superficially acquainted with the Latin and Greek authors, and totally destitute of all other science.—General ideas, and the habits of mankind, have certainly undergone a great revolution; it is proper, therefore, that modes of education should vary, under skilful and prudent direction. Instructions should be taken from every quarter, and the work of improvement begun, without further loss of time. The misfortune however is, that to reform a College would be a thirteenth labour for Hercules. The cleansing the stable of King Augeas, which

which held three thousand oxen, and had not been emptied for thirty years, was, compared with this, but a boyish achievement.—The revenue of this College is very moderate; and the pension, which provides every thing, is but of twenty pounds per annum.

The Priests from this house are the most numerous, and from them I principally drew those outlines of sacerdotal character, which the reader already has seen. They are open, disinterested, religious, and laborious; steady in the discharge of their duties, fond of their profession, and emulous of supporting the character of primitive Churchmen: But they are austere in their principles, confined in their ideas, ignorant of the world, and unpleasant in their manners.

The Clergy have also other seminaries, of inferior distinction, at Paris, at Valladolid in Old Castile, at Rome, and at Lisbon. The number of students in these places is inconsiderable. The distance from England is great, and, abstracting from the expence of so long a journey, parents are not inclined to send their children so far

far from home. The design of all these establishments is solely to educate Churchmen. At Paris are many opportunities of improvement, which that learned University supplies. The mode of education in the other houses is copied from that of Douay; and their Priests, barring the local peculiarities they contract, are greatly in the same model. It is surely time to give new life to this antiquated form: But we want an artist bold enough to attempt it. When Prometheus had kneaded into shape his man of clay, he stole fire from Heaven to animate it.

Whilst the Jesuits stood, St. Omer was their great school for classical improvement; and they supplied England with many able and active Churchmen. At the expulsion of that body from France, their College was given to the Clergy of Douay: In whose hands it now is; but it answers little purpose. English Catholics are not sufficiently numerous to supply scholars for so many houses.—The Jesuits themselves first retired to Bruges, in the Austrian Netherlands, where they opened another College; but, on their total suppression a few years after, that house also

was

was diſſolved, together with every other foundation they poſſeſſed. They then erected an Academy at Liege, (for their ſpirit of enterprize was not to be broken) under the protection of the Biſhop and Prince of that place. They are now no longer Jeſuits; but their Academy is in great eſtimation, and the children of our Catholic gentry principally reſort thither for education. However, as their object is not to form Churchmen, (for they think the Church has uſed them ill) but to inſtruct youth in the faſhionable arts of poliſhed life, the order of Aaron will receive little aſſiſtance from their labours.

The Monks of the order of Saint Benedict have alſo houſes abroad, and their Prieſts come to England. There are four Convents now belonging to them, three in France, and one in Germany, but their numbers are ſmall. In that at Douay is a ſchool for claſſical education, where are generally about thirty ſtudents. From theſe different places but few Prieſts return to England; it being an eſſential part of the Monkiſh inſtitute to keep choir, for which buſineſs a conſiderable number of ſtout lungs is requiſite.

The

The Friars of the order of Saint Francis have likewise a Convent at Douay, which supplies some Priests. Within these few years, they have greatly decreased, owing to the wise regulations France has adopted for the reduction of religious orders, as also because the true spirit of Friarism is much abated. The source likewise, from which formerly they drew a competent subsistence, is almost dried up; I mean the liberal contributions of the public. It begins to be a prevailing notion, that the earthly substance of families can be expended to better purpose, than in maintaining men, who have no return to make to their benefactors, but a promise of a place in paradise, which, it is now discovered, they cannot dispose of; and whose lives, though really more regular than represented, seem not to merit such partial indulgence.

There is also a third order, which now seems rather to increase. The Dominicans, since the suppression of the Jesuits, have grown into more visible form: They have a school near Brussels, and a small Convent at Louvain, in the Austrian territories. Some Priests of this order are likewise in England.

Such is the present state of Catholic establishments abroad, and from them come all the Churchmen at this day in England. It is rather a motley congregation; and they are, and ever have been, much divided by local prejudices of education, views of interest, low jealousies, pretensions to partial favour, and the jars of such selfish passions, as have long had prescriptive possession of the breasts of Churchmen. It would be well, if with their cassocks, their cowls, and their capuches, they would also leave behind them the weaknesses just mentioned, and honestly unite in one christian plan of serving their neighbour, and of discharging the several duties of religion.—It was in these seminaries that was chiefly kept alive that Jacobitical folly, which, like an *ignis fatuus*, led the Catholics of England almost to the brink of ruin. It cannot raise surprise, because it is an obvious effect of circumstances, but it is morally impossible that, whilst this system of foreign education continues, English Catholics can entertain the proper notions of Englishmen.

Englishmen. They must contract something of the manners, and something, I fear, of the principles of those countries, which give them so hospitable a retreat. Yet this effect is by no means so sensible, as from speculation one is induced to believe. The return is not very grateful, but it is observable, that our English boys never lose that antipathy to Frenchmen and French manners, which, I trust, is constitutionally innate. They are, however, greatly exposed, and the experiment should not be tried. It is surely as impolitic, as it is cruel, to retain those penal statutes, by which British subjects are compelled to implore the protection of France, or to deny education to their own children!

THE Ladies would be displeased, were I to take no notice of their foreign establishments. At the time that houses of refuge were provided for the men, whom persecution forced from home, some Ladies of singular zeal, who had also retired from England, attempted to form communities; and their success was great. At this day, the English Nunneries abroad are

Their Nunneries.

are no less than twenty-one. France and the Low Countries have almost the whole number. It is incredible, how they have been able to support themselves; for tho' in many houses their numbers are very thin, yet they go on, braving all the storms of adverse fortune. A high opinion of monastic perfection, fondness for the veil, and, above all, a thought that they suffer on account of religion, are the charms which have filled their cloisters; or at least have preserved them from ruin. It is a misfortune, that England should be deprived of so many fair examples of virtue: Their presence would surely be productive of more real advantage, than their absence; though we have all great confidence in their prayers.—To them our young Ladies are sent for education: Some never return, joining themselves to the holy choirs of virgins; and the few, who are given to the world, become the forlorn hope of the Catholic cause.— Nuns are ill-adapted to the business of education, when this is supposed to consist of precepts and general instruction, with which they cannot be acquainted. Having retired from the world, before they knew it, inspiration only can teach them

them the art of preparing others for its important occupations. Yet this they profess to do, or, in the capacity of instructors, they profess nothing.

Sensible as I am, that no mode of education can be less adapted to improve the mind, and to instil such principles as may form it to the business of life, yet so it happens, that few Ladies have higher pretentions to the palm of female perfection, than have many of the Catholic persuasion. The public knows the truth of this observation. A display of their characters would, I know, offend their modesty; otherwise I would say, that as wives, as mothers, as citizens, and as christians, they stand unrivalled. One is sometimes tempted to suspect that, in molding the soft texture of their minds, nature, too kindly partial, threw in some elements, which otherwise might have fallen to the share of their husbands.—The instructions of the cloister are not favourable to the growth of their virtues; but it is usual with us, not to expose them to public notice, which often blasts the early flower, till maturer age has ripened them into more secure perfection. To this circumstance I principally ascribe

ascribe an effect, which otherwise cannot be accounted for.

If my advice might be followed, I would propose, if Nuns must be, that, after some years of holy retirement, they would return, with missionary powers, to this land of heretics: Their preaching would make more proselytes than a legion of Friars; and their example would be a fair path for us all to walk in.—The Legislature will at last surely relax those Gothic laws, which send into exile so many of their amiable fellow-subjects. Could they receive proper education at home, their thoughts would never turn to cloisters; and if, in lieu, they make it high treason against the state to put on the monastic veil, at least before the age of fifty, it will be a favour done to the rising generation of English Catholics.

Conclusion. IT is time to close this short *view* of English Catholics. I have said whatever seemed necessary on the subject; and I have said it freely. I pretend not to think myself void of all partiality, because I pretend not to be divested of human feelings;

feelings; but of this I am confident, that partiality to my own persuasion has not prevailed on me, to conceal any truth, to disguise any error, or to throw a veil over any weakness. I have blamed where I thought it reasonable; and I have praised where there was merit. Throughout it was my object to support the character of a candid plain-speaking man. If either Catholics or Protestants take offence, it will not give me one uneasy thought. I shall pity men, whose eyes are too weak to bear the impression of Truth, however serene the medium may be, through which it passes. I could have entered into more minute details; and I could have given a much wider span to my reflections; but I thought an object, contracted to a smaller point, was best adapted to produce the effect, I had in view.

It was my design to demonstrate, that neither Church nor State had any thing to fear from English Catholics: and to this end, I brought forward every species of materials, which my sources of information could supply, and which had any tendency to illustrate the point. I described the Catholics as they really are; and

from

from this description if it be not evident to the weakest sight, *that all is secure*, there must be a timidity in Englishmen, that will shudder at the most feeble suggestions of fancy. It is related, I think, as an instance of singular phrenzy in the heroic Ajax, that he took a flock of sheep for a host of enemies: The imagination of the Poet is realized in the conduct of Great-Britain. For two whole centuries, we have been harmless and unoffending; and at the present hour, were an occasion offered, there is not a hand amongst us which would be raised, but in defence of his country.

Things being so, there is but one inference; and this is, That the cry, which was lately heard, and which is industriously kept up, was the cry of malevolence or fanaticism; and that the laws which, like the naked sword over the head of Democles, are held out against us, are cruel, unjust, and tyrannical.—It has been seen, that no just cause was ever given to provoke the enaction of such laws: But now even that plea subsists no longer, by which the multitude was deluded, and the bad designs of party were screened from detection. It is

not

not said, that we are in actual conspiracy against the state, and that schemes of assassination are formed; but it is still said, and it is still believed, that our principles have a natural tendency to such dark works; and that it is not from want of will, but of power, that we do not attempt to place the crown of this realm on the head of a tyrant, or to add it to the triple Tiara of the Roman Pontiff. *Pudet hæc opprobria vobis:* I am really ashamed in the reflection, that men can now be weak enough to indulge such fancies, or can allow themselves the liberty of such childish language. If the view of these absurdities raises my indignation, it is an honest indignation, which becomes me; and I would rather have four legs, and feed on grass, than not freely censure, what I think is an oppression of innocence, and a degradation of human reason. The conduct of Catholics is irreproachable; they profess the most sincere attachment to the civil constitution of this realm; they reprobate the most distant belief of such doctrines as are laid to their charge: Still they are not believed; still the same accusations are repeated; still, under the weak pretence of holding such tenets, they are oppreſſed; and ſtill the ſame infamous code of laws is permitted to remain in full force againſt them!

It might be expected, that the eyes of this nation ſhould now open to the humane and Chriſtian doctrine of general Toleration, on the moſt extenſive plan. They ſhould ſet an example to the other kingdoms of the earth. If we really are that enlightened, that liberal, that humane, that philoſophic people, which we ſo often affect to ſtyle ourſelves, our own conduct at leaſt ſhould not give the firſt lie to the language of our lips.—My ideas are not perhaps adapted to the preſent ſtate of received notions; I believe, they are only fitted to the meridian of Utopia; but had I the power, I would give the utmoſt latitude of profeſſion and practice to all religions, which have votaries in any part of the terraqueous globe. Not only the followers of Mahomet, and the deluded children of Moſes, ſhould not be moleſted, but they ſhould be encouraged to come amongſt us; and the Sun of England ſhould ſhine with equal rays on all the deſcendants of Adam. It is only in ſuch circumſtances that Truth can fairly exert her native powers. Allow all men to think freely, and to act consistently with what they think; and it cannot be, but truth must prevail over error. There would then be no motive for the disguise of sentiments; the mind would receive no undue bias; views of interest would not warp our conceptions; but plain, genuine, unadorned truth would present herself in all her amiable and divine simplicity of form: Religion, with its attendant virtues, would challenge our first belief; and the religion of our choice would *necessarily* be the Christian. Variations in faith might still continue; but these would gradually die away, or at least all distinctions would cease to be odious. The Protestant would sit down by the Catholic; they would discuss, in the language of friendship, their mutual difficulties; and the Gentoo, the Jew, and the Infidel, charmed with a religion, which taught all men to be friends, would earnestly apply to receive instruction in so humane a belief.

I well know such a scheme could not be introduced in the face of an *established Church*; but for that very reason, I would have no religion established by *form of law*.

That mode of faith, which produced the best subjects, should receive peculiar encouragement; and, in the eye of a statesman, this circumstance alone should be the test of its superior excellence. In any other view, the mixing of politics in the concerns of religion, and the granting exclusive favours to a national Church, have ever produced much evil, and never any good. It has confounded objects, in themselves essentially distinct; it has encouraged the growth of every selfish passion; and it has put a bar to the exertions of sincere, honest, and unpliant virtue. The influence of religious worship over the morals and manners of mankind, has made it necessary, it is said, for politicians to court the interest and good-will of Churchmen: They have therefore granted peculiar privileges to some leading sects, and have established their belief by the firm sanction of law: "You only, said they, shall partake of the loaves and fishes."—This certainly is a very confined and mistaken notion. Where can be the policy of an arrangement which, by granting partial favours, secures indeed the attachment of one party, but which forfeits the esteem of the reſt, by a denial of privileges to which all have an equal right?

But without inſiſting on theſe ideas of general juſtice, general humanity, and general policy; can any reaſon be now aſſigned, why Catholics ſhould not enjoy the common rights of Toleration? What is given to other Diſſenters, ſhould be given to them—becauſe they deſerve it. Still, however, I am willing to make ſome allowance to the prejudices of the multitude. The name of *Papyſt* is odious to them, and as long as this impreſſion laſts, it would be wrong to inſult their feelings. As members of ſociety, it is our duty to labour, that abuſes be corrected, that errors be removed, that miſtakes be rectified, and that no man ſuffer wrongfully. The prejudices of the vulgar, and their idle alarms, would ſoon die away, were theſe objects attended to by thoſe, whoſe care it is to inſtruct and to educate. But it is the endeavour rather of theſe men, not to mitigate acrimony and to ſoften prejudice, but to aggravate and to encreaſe both, by malevolent aſperſions and the repetition of declamatory invectives. Would Engliſh Proteſtants openly avow

their

their sentiments; would they say, as do their amiable Scottish brethren, that they mean to persecute and to exterminate the small remains of Popery; we should not be at a loss what plan to adopt. I would rather retire to the frozen regions of Siberia, which would receive me with more hospitality, and where I could think and act with the freedom of a man.—It is not our desire to be put on a level with other subjects; because, in the year 1780, Britain is not sufficiently enlightened to view all men with an equal eye: We shall be satisfied in the least and the lowest condition.—I mean not to point out such measures, as might seem best adapted to give us relief. The penal laws against us should surely be repealed. Let parliament then adopt that plan, which may at once quiet the nation, in their fears of the growth of Popery, and may give that indulgence to Catholics, which, as good and as loyal subjects, they are privileged to expect.

FINIS.

Lately published in Octavo,

And sold by G. ROBINSON, Pater-noster-Row, London,

Letters on *Materialism*, and on *Hartley's Theory of the Human Mind.*—Price 3s.

Immaterialism delineated; or, *A View of the first Principles of Things.*—Price 5s.

A Letter to Dr. Fordyce, on *the delusive and persecuting Spirit of Popery.*—Price 1s. 6d.

www.ingramcontent.com/pod-product-compliance
Lightning Source LLC
Chambersburg PA
CBHW021730220426
43662CB00008B/777